BROTHERS

BROTHERS

the oldest,
the quietest,
the realest,
the farthest,
the nicest,
the fastest,
  & I

Bart Moeyaert

VIGNETTES BY
Gerda Dendooven

TRANSLATED FROM THE FLEMISH BY
Wanda Boeke

FRONT STREET
Asheville, North Carolina

Also by Bart Moeyaert:

Bare Hands

Hornet's Nest

It's Love We Don't Understand

Copyright © 2000 by Bart Moeyaert
Illustrations copyright © 2000 by Gerda Dendooven
English translation copyright © 2005 by Wanda J. Boeke
First published in the Netherlands under the title
Broere by E.M. Querido's Uitgeverij B.B.
All rights reserved
Designed by Helen Robinson
Printed in China

LIBRARY OF CONGRESS CATALOGING-IN-PUBLICATION DATA
Moeyaert, Bart.
[Broere. English]
Brothers: the oldest, the quietest, the realest, the farthest, the nicest,
the fastest, and I / Bart Moeyaert; translated from the Flemish by
Wanda J. Boeke; with vignettes by Gerda Dendooven.
p. cm.
ISBN 1-932425-18-7 (alk. paper)
I. Boeke, Wanda. II. Dendooven, Gerda, ill. III. Title.
PZ7.M7227Br 2005
2004028870

FRONT STREET
An Imprint of Boyds Mills Press, Inc.
A Highlights Company

BROTHERS

CONTENTS

Natural	9
Pipe	13
Slowly	17
Nothing, Nowhere	21
Spring	24
Big Is Nothing	28
Ground	32
Peerdekadoes	35
As Long As We're Healthy	39
Careful	43
Miss Stevens	47
God Bless	51
Swimming Pool	54
Inventions	58
The King Stopped By	62
Robbery	65
Being Good	68
Swarm	72
Punishment	77
Seldom	81
Fat Mène	84

CONTENTS

Standstill	88
Memée	92
Pit	96
The Only Way	100
Under the Sea	104
The Darkness There	107
Patience	111
The Fire	115
Hunderd	119
Back Seat	122
Just Look It Up	126
Sprats and Tripe	129
Back to Normal	132
Losing	135
One Brother with a Long Name	139
Yes, No	143
Jaundice	147
Quiet	150
Loose Change	153
The Creature	157
The Warm Girl	160

NATURAL

My brother and I were in bed trying to get our bodies to lie right. That night we couldn't manage to sleep because there was so much in our heads. We had had a busy day. We'd done all kinds of things but hadn't thought a lot, and we wanted to make up for that before we went to sleep. In the dark we rolled over, on our backs, our sides, our stomachs, our sides, as if we were lying there simmering in our thoughts. There seemed to be no end to it, until my brother asked me in the dark if I knew why it sometimes happened that his ear whistled.

"I didn't know that your ear whistles sometimes," I said. "Myself, I never heard your ear whistle. At least, I can't remember that happening."

My brother said that that didn't surprise him. "Other people can't hear the whistling. I'm the only one, and it scares me every time. What would you do if somebody somewhere was dancing on your future grave again?"

Because I was lying on my stomach and one of my ears was buried in my pillow, I only half heard what my brother was saying. It took a while before I put his sentences together right, and when I had thought more deeply about his future grave, I sat up with a start.

"Are you sure about the grave part?" I asked. I widened my eyes to be able to see my brother in the dark, but I couldn't.

"It's not something you know for sure," said my brother. "It's something you've known for a long time. A kind of natural, innate belief. Something old that was given to you at birth: when there's a whistling in your ear, somebody's dancing on your future grave."

"So, how come I don't know that?" I asked. I threw back the blanket, looked on the cold linoleum with my feet for my slippers but didn't find them, and then tiptoed to the other room, where my other brothers slept. It turned out that they were awake too. When they heard the sticky sound of my steps on the linoleum, they sat up and switched on the bedside lamp. They asked what was wrong, with a look that said they hoped a lot was wrong.

I asked them if their ears ever whistled and if they knew what went on at the very same moment. I held my breath for a little bit longer, because my brothers probably wanted some time to think, but they didn't. They came right out and said that their ears whistled regularly, and that at the very same moment somebody was dancing on their future graves. Then they looked my way with that slightly glassy-eyed look they often had. Then I always knew that I was young, very young, even—the youngest, really.

"You mean those ears of yours have never whistled?" asked my brother.

"No," I said. "Never. At least, not that I know of."

My brothers exchanged glances, looked at my ears again, and made motions with their eyebrows.

One of my brothers raised his hand. He said, "Wait a minute. You don't mean to tell me that, um, your left hand hasn't ever itched before?"

"Or your right hand?" asked another brother.

I shook my head and shrugged my shoulders.

"If your left hand itches, you're going to make money," said my one brother.

"And if your right hand itches, you'll lose it," said my other brother. "That's the way it is. On the left, filthy rich; on the right, not a stitch."

My breath caught in the back of my throat. I looked at my hands, which to my knowledge had never yet itched. This was likely the case, because very rich I wasn't yet, and much loss I hadn't yet suffered.

"And all of you just know this?" I said. "Why didn't anybody ever tell me?"

"It's something you don't have to be told," my brothers said at the same time.

"It's in everybody's genes. A kind of natural belief."

"Just like everybody already knows before they're born that somebody's gossiping about you if your ears ring loudly," said one brother.

"Or burn," said my other brothers. "They can burn, too. And flap. It's all the same. Then you're being talked about."

I couldn't stand still anymore. I'd never heard so many new things one right after the other like that. Everything I had always known from before I was born suddenly started happening at the same time. My ears whistled, my left hand itched, my right hand too, and my ears flapped and caught on fire.

I looked at my brothers, at the oldest, the quietest, the realest, the farthest, the nicest, and the fastest. They all sat there scratching their noses.

"No, no, no!" I exclaimed. "I bet this means something too? If your nose itches?"

"Yes," said my brothers. "Somebody's thinking about us."

And it was true. At that moment our father came into the room. He was thinking about us and smacked us on the head so that our ears whistled and continued to burn for a long time after that.

PIPE

Our father had a pipe that helped him think. The pipe hung on a hook inside his mouth, always the same corner, so that our father had his hands free for a glass or a book or a pen. Out of Father's mouth and out of the bowl of the pipe, smoke curled up, always the same bluish smoke that would stand around my father like a separate room.

We would walk like thieves past his chair when he was smoking. We kept our distance from the tobacco that crowded in on us, but were particularly afraid of the way he smoked. His eyes looked blurry, like the walls of his little room. His expression was directed more inside than out.

Studying, my mother called it. He's catching up on his learning. And then she would beg us to walk through the room as little as possible, and at the very least try to be quiet, because if we interrupted our father's thinking, he'd lose his train of thought and would have to start all over again and maybe never get back to the point he had been at before.

We had already discovered for ourselves how strangely thoughts can jump around, but it was beyond us that our mother called our father's smoking studying. If somebody else were to sit in a chair for an hour with a pipe, our mother would say he wasn't doing anything. Go do something, she'd say.

"And yet, that's the way it is," said our mother. "The pipe helps your father think, and for him, thinking is the same as studying."

We looked from the kitchen into the living room through the serving hatch and saw our father sitting there studying. With one side of his mouth he imitated the sound of a dripping faucet. At each drop, smoke escaped. To me, it was an escaping thought each time. A thought that had become one too many in his head.

We had our doubts about what our mother said. We wanted to see proof, but had to admit that our father never sat in his den of smoke longer than the time it took to smoke one pipe. In the end he would always scratch the pipe that had gone out with a little spoon into the ashtray on the side table, cough once, and then disappear into his real study without a word. No smoke hung there, just silence. We could hear the wheels of his desk chair squeak all the way in the kitchen and knew that that would be the last we would hear of our father. He would continue with his writing of a new textbook for children who knew nothing about long ago.

It kept my brothers and me busy. One time we went and stood around the ashtray and looked at the wad that our father had spooned out of the pipe. One side of the wad was ashes, but the other side had tobacco that could still be used.

My brother looked up and said that there were still a few

chestnuts lying around in his room. My other brother also looked up and said that he had a sharp knife, and yet another brother was willing to volunteer his ballpoint pens for the day. They looked at one another, moved their eyebrows up and down, and the three of them began sniggering and whispering among themselves. They fished the wad of tobacco out of the ashtray.

My other brothers and I sighed. We could puzzle things out. We weren't stupid. We already knew before we were sitting in our hut behind the garden shed what we were going to do.

"We're going to investigate," said my brother.

"We're going to investigate what a pipe does to the brain," said my other brother.

The wild chestnuts they had brought along they hollowed out on one side, and into the side they drilled a hole where the empty plastic holder of a ballpoint pen would fit.

"Handmade, they don't have to look great," said my brother. "A pipe is mostly supposed to draw well, because if it doesn't, you're paying more attention to your breathing than to your thoughts, and then you still won't have shown that you can catch up on learning with a pipe, or think better."

Of the seven pipes we had made, he was forced to choose one, since we had enough tobacco for only one pipe.

"We should have thought of that earlier," said my brother.

"As long as you haven't lit up a pipe, you can't catch up on learning anything," said my other brother. "Come on, go investigate just once."

15

Even before dinnertime, he went to investigate. He hung the pipe in the corner of his mouth, held a match to it, and after a little while made exactly the same sounds as our father. Meanwhile, we asked him if it was working, but he only mumbled and moaned, indisputably like somebody whose mind is elsewhere, completely preoccupied by his own thoughts. He was catching up on a lot of learning, in my opinion, because his eyes kept getting blurrier, and around his head the walls of his study kept getting thicker. He kept on smoking until our mother called us for dinner.

Then my brother even took the time to knock the ash out of the chestnut and to cough a little. After that, he crossed the yard without a word as we followed him with our eyes. The similarity to our father was striking. We knew that we wouldn't see him at the dinner table. We were convinced that he had caught up on some kind of learning with the pipe, something that he had to digest all by himself—just like our father did—in a place where silence reigned.

SLOWLY

When we had finished dinner, our mother said that it had happened too fast. Could we even remember what we'd shoved down our gullets? We looked at our mother in a panic, picked our knives and forks off our plates, and looked under them to see if there were any remains of what we had eaten. There wasn't a trace. We had already licked our plates clean.

My one brother exclaimed that we'd eaten sausage, or wait a minute, no, meatballs, and then we all tried to say something. Our mother looked at the meat that we were making up, the vegetables that came out of our mouths in words, and shook her head. She said we were dreadful boys.

For punishment we got clean plates. We had to keep our mouths shut and sit there while our mother sang and walked back and forth between the kitchen and the table. She cleared away the large silverware, laid small forks and knives on the table, and wove an end to her made-up song.

"Now we're all going to start over again," she said as she placed a tray full of bowls and platters on the table. "All over again and slowly." She nodded and made circles in the air above the tray.

17

We looked at what was in the bowls and on the platters. There were desserts in kinds and sizes we had never seen before. Our jaws dropped in surprise. One brother almost slipped off the edge of his seat, and another brother, who almost never said anything, made a humming sound.

Our mother was a fairy queen. She pointed at the cake and the pastry and the cookies and gave them names that, in our opinion, she was making up on the spot. She poked her fork into the poor knight fruit toasts and the just-as-much cupcakes. She said that there were day brothers on one of the platters and on the others chatterbox lace cookies and fat cats. She looked as if she believed this herself.

We shook our heads and said, "Mother, whatever they're called, we're never going to be able to eat them all."

"We will if we eat slowly," she said. "We have to learn how. With cakes and pastry there's no sauce, so we can't wash them down that way. We shouldn't mix what's on our plates. Things will go into our mouths separately, and we will chew before we swallow, because a piece of fruitcake can't go down the hatch crosswise."

We remained on guard. My brothers and I had the feeling that our mother was saying something different from what she was actually saying, but we didn't know what.

She sat at the table looking around contentedly, from my oldest brother on one side of her to me on the other side, and then allowed her hand to drift over to the platter of poor knights. She placed one on her plate, cut off a piece, popped it into her mouth, and made chewing movements.

Our jaws slowly went up and down as we watched. We chewed on our tongues and, after a while, on our thickened saliva, because our mouths were watering. Our mother looked so enraptured, she was so enjoying that one piece of pastry, that we all suddenly wanted to try.

Without a second thought we threw ourselves over the table, groped around in the bowl of chatterboxes, and snatched handfuls of day brothers from the platter. My mother swallowed just in time, because before we were able to stuff anything into our mouths, she cried, "Slowly!"

That was what we'd forgotten. Whatever we held in our hands we put on our plates and looked at guiltily.

"For heaven's sake!" exclaimed our mother.

We nodded more slowly than we usually did and kept looking at our plates. Hello, chatterbox, we thought. Hello, just-as-much, fat cat.

We mashed something with our forks. We cut a piece of pastry, broke off a piece of candied fruitcake, and brought it separately to our mouths. We didn't swallow right away but first moved our tongue and our jaws. The sweetness of honey sought the tip of our tongues, the creamy tartness stayed on the edge, the bitterness prickled in back, and the pieces of almond did everything at the same time and all over. We leaned back in our chairs in rapture while swallowing, because we had never experienced this before.

"We've never experienced this before," we said to our mother.

"Then I'm happy for you," she said.

"From now on, we'll always eat slowly," we promised. "Word of honor!"

"Then I'm happy for me," said our mother. "Everything's always tastier eaten more slowly."

We slowly emptied the platters and the bowls and thought that we would forever keep our promise. In the evening, we enjoyed our brown bread sandwiches longer and more. We understood better the next morning why a soft-boiled egg tastes nice for breakfast.

But soon enough we saw that our mother had misled us.

"I'm so proud of how slow you all are," said our mother that afternoon above the steaming pots that were on the table.

To be on the safe side, we thanked her for her compliment.

"Rest assured, Mother," we said, "eating slowly is not a problem for us." After which we tried to smile with bone-dry pork liver in our mouths, and under our tongues, plump Brussels sprouts that, as soon as our mother wasn't looking, we swallowed whole.

NOTHING, NOWHERE

One night my one brother crawled into bed cold. The chill lingered in his pajamas, and his breath also came from outside.

"Where were you?" I asked when he finally lay still.

"Nowhere," he said.

"Well, it's cold there," I said, and I shivered.

He didn't answer.

I waited until his breathing slowed, but there was still nothing, even after that. He rolled onto his side. It became so quiet in the room that it seemed as if my brother had stopped existing. He didn't scratch himself anymore, didn't rub his feet to warm them, didn't curl up like a cat the way he always did. I lay for a long time, waiting for a sound, any sound, but nothing stirred. Everything was asleep, absolutely everything—the neighbor's dog, the neighbors themselves, all the cars for miles around, the wind, and because of that the trees around the house too. Nothing rustled, nothing sighed, nothing droned.

I was just about to ask again where my brother had been, when the stairs creaked. I knew exactly which step it was, the first one after the landing, and which doorknob rattled,

I knew that as well. I sat up in bed, looked in the direction of the door to our room, and in the twilight watched my other brother, bent over like a thief, sneak to his bed. He didn't even do it by feel, just slipped between the sheets in almost a single motion.

I wasn't wrong. Just like my one brother, he had brought the cold in with him.

"Where were you?" I asked when he was lying down.

"Nowhere," he said.

"Nowhere," I said, and I rubbed my arms to get my goose bumps to go away. I kept staring in the direction of his bed on purpose because he would have to feel my gaze and would have to say something after a while anyway, just to be rid of me, but he wasn't bothered by anything. He remained silent as if he were already asleep and had never been awake, and now, with his lips sealed, he said that I was a dreamer, had a lot of imagination, but it really saw nothing but flies.

I needed a lot of time before I realized that I was sitting up in bed with a pounding heart, waiting for something that didn't come, and hearing a hiss in my ears because it was so quiet everywhere. This was the middle of the night, I knew. This was what the darkest hours of the night looked like. On the other side of the world, there was light and movement. There, they were now walking to work in their sneakers, eating cake with a hole in the middle for breakfast, a subway came ding-dinging out of the ground, but here, on this side, everything had been brought to a halt, and whatever wasn't sleeping wasn't supposed to see the light of day.

I opened my eyes wider. Because I tried not to think of what lurked under my bed at night or behind the curtains, I started to see the worst before me, and it was in every corner of the room. It had claws, it grinned, it moved like a spider, sideways. Soon I would hear the clicking of eight paws on the linoleum.

As slowly as I could, I lay back down. I pressed my head into my pillow so I wouldn't have to hear anything, arranged my back against the mattress as if for shelter, and pulled my heavy blanket over me. Only after a couple of seconds did I dare to breathe in, quietly now, quietly.

Until the stairs creaked again.

In my mind, I was catapulted by a spring and sat up. I was all ears for what was happening in the little hallway. I heard two brothers giggling. They were laughing so hard that they held on to each other with one hand and held each other's mouths shut with the other, that's what it sounded like, because they were about to burst out laughing if they didn't watch out.

Through a crack in the door, they let a little bit of chill in.

One brother said, "Again tomorrow?"

"Yes, again tomorrow," whispered my brothers, who weren't at all asleep yet.

I looked from one to the other in the semidarkness.

I said, "What again tomorrow?"

It was silent, as if it startled them that I was still alive.

Then they said, "Nothing, nothing." And they were aware of nothing.

SPRING

When the time came to throw open the windows of the houses and hang out the blankets, my brothers and I would grow restless. It was time for Memée to remark, as she did every year, that winter was a sly season, by which she meant that life had moved on quietly for a few months, its little turns inconspicuous, but it had moved on nevertheless. The neighbor lady would claim, as she did every year, that this winter again many old people had died in their sleep. And in a few weeks we would feel the urge to find out once and for all if it was really true that rats pulled ducklings underwater.

Winter was over.

First it was time for spring cleaning, announced by our mother and Memée with the purchase of a chamois cloth, rubber overshoes, and new aprons from the market. We had to prepare ourselves for dust and suds and drafts. We could expect grumbling for a week about where, for heaven's sake, did all this junk come from and that it was shameful that in this house we couldn't just go up to the attic but had to clamber over a mountain first. Why were we the kind of people who never threw anything away?

We bowed our heads even before Memée and our mother

started grumbling. We admitted that we were that kind of people, without their having said anything.

"But sometimes junk just *seems* like junk," we would observe. "That bag of springs is part of something big, those little metal things won't stay metal things, and that orange crate may look like an orange crate, but it's a piece of something that's going to be built. Soon."

And we were not lying. When spring cleaning came around, there was always a moment when we would sit up in bed and express our longings. These were usually longings we could grab hold of, like a bike, a fishing rod, or a train that ran on batteries. The things we named always lay within arm's reach. It wasn't inconceivable that we would someday get hold of a bike or a rod or a train, because when all the basements and attics in the neighborhood were cleaned out one fine day, people would put the stuff outside in front of their houses or front fences, and then the city truck would come to load everything up. You could never tell if a person might be wanting to get rid of a bike or a rod or a train. That person would watch the garbage truck leave, feeling satisfied because the house was empty again and a person could start all over with nice things.

Up until then it hadn't ever happened. We had never found a bike or a rod or a train in the trash. Longing was a nice feeling, and talking about it was also nice, and to comfort ourselves beforehand, we also discussed, sitting up in bed, the thing that we were most certainly going to find, because we had found it every year until now.

The neighbor lady and Memée had reassured us once again. Yes, many old people had died in their sleep, and yes, winter was a sly season. Even if it did so quietly, life kept going on, with those inconspicuous little turns, but it went on.

We sat in bed imagining where a baby had outgrown its carriage this time, and how this time we would convert the chassis, which we were most certainly going to find in the trash, into a racecar.

"Dee-luxe!" my one brother exclaimed.

We gave him a questioning look: What was he suddenly talking French for? But he had already jumped to his feet and turned into a racecar deluxe, with springs to absorb the bumps and an orange crate for a trunk. The little metal things held together all the loose boards we had found in the trash, and we had even succeeded in converting part of an easy chair into a wide seat. We tore around the turns with the racecar. They were the sharpest of turns. You could tell by our screeching brakes and squealing tires.

"What speed!" my one brother exclaimed. "The red three is entering turn four!"

We all squealed and screeched along with him and imagined at the same time that we'd found half a can of red paint in the trash, and we saw ourselves painting a "3" on the side of our racecar, and we were still seeing this even when my one brother had already crashed into a tree and let himself fall back onto the bed with a lot of commotion.

"Yes!" we exclaimed, and we coughed from all the excitement. "That was a great ride, a great ride!"

"It'll be like that!" said my one brother.

"It can be like that!" said my other brother.

With that observation, we were back on earth.

"We'll see," we said, enjoying the longing. "Some kid somewhere will have outgrown its carriage. Winter is a sly season."

We rolled onto our sides and went to sleep with our minds at rest. If we didn't find a baby carriage, we might find a bike, or a rod, or a train. If worse came to worst, we would have to convert our springs, our orange crate, and our little metal things into rubbish and leave them at the fence. That wasn't all that bad. We'd just go investigate a week earlier whether rats pulled ducklings underwater. It was spring, and you could do all kinds of things.

BIG IS NOTHING

Our father brought us to a city we had never been to before. In the car, he wondered aloud if we weren't too little for so much adventure. The city we were going to was bigger and taller than anything we had ever seen, and the streets had the names of countries and people and were so wide that they seemed like village squares here and there.

"Everything is big there," said our father.

We shrugged our shoulders and said we weren't scared.

"Big is nothing," we said, acting tough. "A city is nothing to be scared of."

"Hmm," went our father. "No, not in the movies. But in reality it's different. In reality the city makes noise. All kinds of things thunder right by. They can pop up suddenly with a clanging behind you and be full of people, or they can disappear with lots of wind into big tunnels."

"We're still not scared," we said.

"That's good," replied our father. "I just wanted to be sure."

He left the highway and drove in the direction of some white buildings in the distance and still more buildings farther away.

"Most of all, a city is lots of stones," said my one brother.

He looked wise as he said this, but he sounded as if he were telling a joke. As if we could expect stones to land on our heads. We had to laugh at him, but there was a crooked edge to our smiles because we realized that in a city a lot could fall out of the sky, it was true.

We hunkered down a bit in the back seat, and at the same time we made our necks long. We really didn't want to miss any of what was happening outside. We had just reached a busy road between tall buildings, with lines of moving cars to the left and lines of moving cars to the right, and it seemed as if our father didn't need to steer anymore, as if our car moved ahead all by itself. It glided more than it drove, went over the rim of a pit that turned out to be a tunnel, and after a few turns reached a basement in a single motion.

Even before we were parked, my brothers and I realized that the city was a labyrinth better not thought about at night in bed. Underground, the city was hollow and stank of gasoline, and above ground the side streets blended into others and there was no end to them.

We clutched the plastic bags that we had all gotten from our mother. There was a little bottle of apple juice and a candy bar inside each one, and an egg-salad sandwich. Most of my brothers had already eaten their candy bar and had started on their apple juice from the thirst.

A couple of brothers and I had been smarter. We still had everything. If we were to get lost, we would not die of hunger and thirst. That thought alone already made us nervous. Our father needed seven hands to hold on to us. We walked in front of his feet, we stepped on his heels, we were happy that he scolded us because we knew that he was close.

"This is the most beautiful square in the country," he said after a time, while we were walking among a lot of people. "It's about two feet higher than it used to be. That sounds funny, but it's true."

Most of all it sounded unnecessary. We stood two feet higher than we used to, but we still couldn't see anything of the square because there were so many long coats standing around us. The coats tried to split us up. It seemed as if they wanted to take our father away from us. They got in the way so much that my brothers and I even began to shout.

"Dad? Dad!"

We were happy that all seven of us reached the curb on the other side and had space to catch our breath. If it had been up to us, we'd have walked back to the car right then, flown up the highway, headed for small, quiet, and few.

But then we saw the mouse. Who saw it first, I don't know, but it's a fact that all seven of us leapt among the long coats and took off after the creature, shouting. The mouse darted every which way and the people scattered in all directions and my brothers and I whooped and shouted, the way we whooped and shouted at home when we chased a mouse. A wave broke over the most beautiful square in the country, and as quickly as the mouse had turned up, it disappeared again.

We scared ourselves. When we looked up, the world had

changed. Our father was still our father, but there were fewer coats walking around and the most beautiful square in the country was more beautiful than we first thought. Not as big either. We said this to one another.

"This square isn't as big as all that," we said, and we furtively glanced at the ground to see if maybe the mouse had heard us.

GROUND

For a plate of sprouts, Brussels sprouts, we bought a piece of ground. A plot measuring three by three feet for a plate of sprouts sounded like a good deal, but my brothers weren't wild about it. They were not into soil, or sprouts. I was, but that didn't count. It was just something different, that's why they made the swap; you never knew what might come of it.

"Choose," said our father. "Which plot is worth the sprouts? A plot with grass on it or a plot with flowers or a plot that's just a plot?"

My brothers looked at one another and smacked their lips. They chose the plot with flowers on it.

That surprised me. Why didn't they choose the plot with grass on it, a rabbit could live there. Or why didn't they choose the plot that was just a plot? All kinds of things could still grow on it; one part could be grass for the rabbit and one part for flowers to make it look nice, if they wanted.

That might be true, but my brothers had a nose for business. They drew a square in the flowerbed and said, "This plot."

"This one?" said our father. "Done. That'll be the one then. It's tall and deep and all yours."

"Yes," said my brothers. "Yes," I said, and we walked inside because we still had plates to empty.

My one brother said we needed scissors, we had harvesting to do.

"Harvesting?" I asked.

"Yes, harvesting," said my brothers. "Picking fruits." And they shook their heads and rolled their eyes. How was it possible, such a big forehead and still such a little brain?

They harvested the daisies. They rolled them up ten at a time in old newspapers and sold them door-to-door. They said it was for the poor children, and they weren't lying. We didn't have any money of our own.

The last bunch my brothers sold to Focke. They had figured that right—it was steps saved. They had to go to Focke's anyway.

Focke's wife pulled a box of seeds out from among the vegetables and fruit and let my brothers rummage through it. From the box they chose a big packet with a container of garden cress sprouts printed on it and a little packet with a picture of parsley in a basket.

"Good seed for healthy plants," Focke himself said.

"We hope so," said my brothers.

We went home, walked in through the front door and out through the back, to our piece of ground.

"Sow," said my brothers.

They drew a pillar up to the sky. After that, they threw down their hands as if only with force could they show how far under the ground our land went. Everything right below us was ours, down to the fire in the earth. Everything above our heads was ours, infinity plus a mile.

I said that I'd never thought you bought so much ground and so much air when you bought land.

"Yes, yes," said my brothers. "But the seed will still only fall on one single spot between the two. Here." And they pointed at our plot of land, three by three feet.

They sowed the garden cress and the parsley like brown sugar and emptied the full watering can.

With their arms folded, they stood around our land and watched as the water slowly drained away. The ground bubbled here and there. It was nice to see.

I pointed at the smell that rose up off the soil and entered your nose. It was the smell of greenery and wood and fertilizer, but my brothers misunderstood. They thought I was pointing at a worm that was drowning.

"Movement," said my one brother.

"Spectacle," said my other brother.

They all had to laugh, particularly because my one brother had never seen a flying worm before.

"Heave-ho!" they cried.

After that they went off to play soccer. After that they went fishing. After that they blew up a frog. And after that they did even more things with fast results. They shouted from far away, wondering whether there was anything to be seen yet.

"Not yet," I said, but I didn't tell them that I heard the cress shooting up. I stroked the soil with our rake, and now and then I stood with one foot on our piece of ground, in our own air.

One morning our father said that we had to go to Gaby's. He had ordered a peerdekadoes from her, and it was to have been baked the night before, without raisins.

We looked at our father, why he was saying that so emphatically, and he waved his hand next to his head and smiled out of one corner of his mouth. Obviously we had never eaten peerdekadoes with raisins, he said, or we'd have known that it's even more disgusting than groats. Without raisins—now that's when it becomes food for the gods.

We all had to laugh.

"Is that funny?" asked our father.

We said no. We pushed on our stomachs and pinched our lips shut with our fingers to squelch our giggling, because it was April 1 and our one brother had just succeeded in tying our father's shoelaces together under the table. Father had no inkling of mischief, and our mother and Memée had no clue, either, and we thought this was great, because at the beginning of breakfast we'd already tied the two of them to their chairs with their bathrobe belts.

"Come on, we're going," my brother said with a red face.

"OK," we said.

Outside, we could hardly even walk. Our arms and legs were weak from laughing. We fell against one another and squeaked, "April Fool's, April Fool's!" and imagined the shocked faces of our father and our mother and Memée and decided we would have to find another couple of April Fool's Days in the year. May 3, or why not June 21?

On the threshold of the bakery, we grew quiet because we had a lot of respect for Gaby. You could tell by her face that she didn't get much sleep. She had bags under her eyes and worries around her mouth. At night she helped her husband, whom we saw only during the afternoon when he made his rounds delivering bread in his little van. Gaby and her baker always worked, and always worked hard. There was no such thing as too much time, so they put no stock in small talk.

"What'll it be?" asked Gaby when we were standing in front of her counter.

"Our father's peerdekadoes," we said.

"His ... huh?" asked Gaby.

"Peerdekadoes," we said. "Without raisins."

My one brother said that our father couldn't come get his order himself because we had tied his shoelaces together. He grinned. "April Fool's, April Fool's!"

We all started snickering again; it was stronger than we were. Even Gaby had to laugh. We could tell by her eyes, which brightened a little.

"Right," she said, and she bit her lip. "The peerdekadoes. Done."

She disappeared through a door behind which was another door. We were just talking about Gaby's feet, that it always seemed as if she walked on the sides of her shoes, when we heard laughter break out behind the two doors. It was Gaby and her baker. It made us happy inside, thinking of the pleasure we were giving them. They thought our prank with our father's shoelaces was just as great as we did.

"Good one, eh? The one we played on our dad," we said when Gaby returned and stood there shaking a little with leftover mirth.

"Yes," she said, "very good," and she laid her hand on the fresh peerdekadoes, which looked to us very much like a loaf of bread, and a very large loaf at that.

"Tell your father it's a good one," said Gaby.

"We'll tell him," we said. "But Father knows that already. He says peerdekadoes without raisins is food for the gods."

"Right," said Gaby, and she wrapped thin paper around the food for the gods and handed it to us over the counter. "Food for the gods."

"Yes. Hooray for Father!" we cried, and we said good-bye to Gaby in our various ways.

Outside, we suddenly lost all our words. We didn't know how it had happened, but all of a sudden we felt like we had to walk as close as possible to the brother who was carrying the peerdekadoes. We stuck our noses up in the air to see if we couldn't catch some of the fresh-baked smell, and rubbed the corners of our mouths dry because there was saliva caught there. The idea that not only our father but Gaby, too, called peerdekadoes without raisins food for the gods, and that we didn't know about it, was unsettling to us.

"You'd swear it was just a loaf of bread," said my one brother.

"But it's a peerdekadoes," said my other brother.

"Without raisins," we breathed in unison. As if by automatic response, we came to a standstill in a circle, our heads bent, with the peerdekadoes in the middle.

"From the top you can't tell that it's good," we said.

"We could try the bottom," said my one brother, and he tore some of the paper on the bottom, applied a little force, and held up a piece of food for the gods, letting it disappear into his mouth right away.

We held our breath.

Even before our brother began to chew, his face brightened. We thought he was melting from the taste, we thought he was going to sing like an angel, but no. He began to shake with laughter and said with his mouth full that it was April Fool's and that he thought Gaby was fabulous.

"Have a taste—white bread!" he cried. "Gaby got our father good!"

And we ran home, roaring "April Fool's! April Fool's!" We were curious as to whether somebody was going to play another joke on us or not. We rubbed our hands together, because the day was still long.

It depended on what kind of onions they were. Pearl onions were too small, shallots didn't amount to anything, and nothing was known about red onions. They had to be yellow farmers' onions, those big ones, the ones our mother put in stews and soup. We peeled them until they were white as snow and smooth, and before we tucked them under our armpits we poked a few holes in them for more effective results.

"Holes?" my one brother asked us.

"For air," said my other brother.

"For moisture," said yet another.

"For more effective results," I said.

A silence fell during which my brothers kept staring at my mouth—maybe something else stupid was going to come out of it. They let me know that words with three syllables were strange when I uttered them. They rolled their eyes, clamped their upper arms over their chests, and shrugged their shoulders stiffly.

"That's the way it is, isn't it?" I asked carefully. "We're poking holes in them for more effective results? With holes, the smell and the moisture come out faster."

"Listen," said my one brother without looking at me,

"it talks. It knows everything about holes in onions, and it talks."

My other brother thought I'd better keep the hole in my face shut.

"We didn't ask for any comments," he said. "You don't have to get sick. We do. We have to get sick, for our own well-being."

"For our own health, really," said my other brother.

I went, "Pfft." I wasn't able to get more out because of my pent-up anger. I had heard the way they emphasized the word "we" and made it more important than anything else in the world. I breathed in and out deeply, tried to think of something else, to become somebody else, because my anger almost came out. I tried growing taller than my brothers. I wanted to watch them from above and find them ridiculous. Just look. Look—tomorrow they have to do all kinds of things at school that they don't want to do, and there they are now with onions under their armpits, waiting for a fever.

My thoughts helped. My brothers suddenly looked just great. All six were trying to move as little as possible. Now and then they let their hands drift to their noses and felt with a careful finger whether their nose was running yet, because besides the onions they were using the wet towel method. Your nose was supposed to start to run from a wet towel on the back of your neck. At the same time they had stuffed their shoes with cardboard, because if you did that, nausea wouldn't be far behind. In no time you'd have symptoms of dehydration. The towel made your nose run and the cardboard sucked the moisture out of your body, and on top of that you also got a fever from the onions. Even the best doctor, it was said, couldn't figure out what illness it was.

I lifted my arms so my onions fell to the floor, I threw off the wet towel, and I bent down to untie my shoes.

"What are you going to do?" asked my brothers.

"Nothing," I said. "All six of you can go ahead and lie in bed. I've had it. I don't have to do what you all have to do tomorrow, so I don't need any onions or a towel, and I don't need any cardboard in my shoes either, although I am starting to feel sick to my stomach."

My brothers looked at me and at one another and then at me again, and felt their cheeks with their fingertips.

"Really sick to your stomach?" asked my brothers.

Maybe I was just a little nauseated by my brothers and by anger, or maybe it was just a coincidence, or, who knows, holes in onions did produce more effective results.

"Yes," I said while I pulled the cardboard, which felt a little clammy, out of one of my shoes and then out of my other shoe. "Don't any of you feel anything yet?"

My brothers looked at their feet. There was nothing to be seen from their feet. I saw them wiggle their toes in the tips of their shoes; I saw them gently give their upper bodies a shake to feel if a drop of sweat was dripping down somewhere; I saw them touch their ears to feel if there wasn't any fever behind them.

"You're all older than I am," I said. "And bigger. So, you'll have to wait longer for results."

At the door, I turned around. Most of my anger had passed. I even felt sorry for my brothers.

"Good luck," I said.

But it didn't help.

That afternoon, our father took my hand and called upstairs to see if anybody was going along to the supermarket, where we always got a treat. At four o'clock, our mother called upstairs to see if anybody wanted any pancakes with brown sugar and apples. And to make it even more fun, visitors who had bought a fast, expensive car came by wanting to take us all for a spin.

My brothers missed all the nice things that happened that day. Early the same evening, I heard twelve onions drop above my head just as the lady who was visiting said that fast and expensive aren't the important things in life. "As long as we're healthy," she said, and she nodded at my brothers as they came in one by one looking tired, it's true, but fine in every other way.

CAREFUL

One time when the weather wasn't fit for man or beast, we were obliged to go outside. We had to.

Before breakfast, Memée was already shuffling back and forth from the front of the house to the back, and at each window she came to, she made binoculars of her hands, and then with her mouth against the glass, she said that it hadn't stopped yet, that it would never stop. What a deluge; the storm drain couldn't possibly keep swallowing it.

The storm drain did keep swallowing it, but it drank less thirstily and more slowly by the hour. After a while, my brothers and I followed Memée, wringing our hands. We made little round panes in the condensation on the windows and tried to look outside. The world was liquid and wind-blown. We predicted wet feet for one another.

To scare ourselves, we put our boots and our coats on indoors, and we tied our hoods tight and buttoned them up. It wouldn't be long before the puddle over the storm drain outside was a lake. A plastic bag and some other rubbish were clogging the grate. We could feel the way the water there churned and sucked; it was churning and sucking inside us, too.

"We'll have to," we said to Memée.

"No," said Memée, and she wrung her hands. "It's too dangerous."

"You don't think we're going to drown, do you?" we said, and we laughed. We acted out how we would drown in the lake over the storm drain and be swept along into the sewer, incredible the way it slurped and gurgled.

"Don't do that," said Memée.

All this time, the clouds had been growling among themselves as if they had throats. Sometimes two bolts of lightning shot down at the same time.

Memée stared into the darkness.

"This is going to be terrible," she said, and she made a muzzle of her hands and gulped air with them. "I feel it in my bones." She pointed at her ears. "I hear it."

We listened, but we didn't know what we were supposed to hear. We didn't feel anything in our bones. Maybe the air was warmer than it had just been. The rain was falling more gently, maybe. It was steadily washing down more than pouring down.

Suddenly it cursed so hard up there we couldn't think another thought. The whole sky was coming down. Whole choirs of angels were thundering down the stairs, and we stood there as if glued to the spot. Our breath rushed into our throats, and it was suddenly steaming under our coats. We hardly had time to blink our wide eyes. What we had seen all morning long was drizzle. A little shower. Clouds that sputtered a little. Now we were getting the rain. It suddenly came down in buckets. A torrential downpour we all watched in silence. The street turned into a river. It gushed and spattered. The tulips were beaten flat, the leaves on the trees blew upside down and stayed that way, the conifers bent farther and farther down.

Memée shuffled backward, to where the wind was blowing the rain against the windowpanes, and began to pray. That was not a good sign. She pointed at the threshold. The water was lapping at it.

She made a sound as if she wanted to spur on a horse and said that we should get her boots and her coat. We were instantly at her side again. We helped her into her coat and into her boots. We almost tied her rain hat on for her. Our hearts pounded in our throats, but our chests were broad. We grew thick mustaches and got a determined look in our eyes. We had to keep Memée on her feet and stand by her in what she was about to do.

"Stay close to me," she said, and she counted to three, but we couldn't hear the three because by then the door was open and we were standing outside and being washed out of our clothes. Memée had a close call and we saw her almost blow away.

"This is terrible!" we shouted at one another, and we stretched all the syllables so that it actually became true. It *was* terrible.

"Stay close to me!" Memée shouted again, and she raised a broom in the air and fought her way to the street against the wind. We fought alongside her. We built a little fort around her and lifted up her feet for her, because the lake over the storm drain had already reached the path beside the house. There was no time to lose.

"Careful!" cried my one brother, and that sounded good. My brothers and I looked around and cautiously shuffled ahead, because we wouldn't be the first ones to disappear into a pool. We held on to Memée by clutching her coat.

"Help me!" she said. "Help!"

She didn't need to ask twice. We all held a little piece of the broom and prodded and shoved and stirred in the lake until we found the grate. Then we formed a snake of brothers. Memée was our head. She bent down with difficulty, fished up a plastic bag and some other rubbish, and passed the booty to us. We cheered, but cheered discreetly.

"Watch out! Behind you!" we shouted, to keep things exciting.

On our way back to the house, we already began describing what we had seen, and we thanked each other because we had saved one another's lives. One brother saw a worm float by, white and puffy. He pointed at it and said that things could have turned out like that.

Whenever Miss Stevens came over, the house shrank. Our father became a midget, our mother didn't weigh a thing, and my brothers and I turned into little birds.

Miss Stevens tried to lie about her size by folding herself double and bending her knees a little, but it never made more than an inch or so of difference. We could tell by looking at her that she would have preferred to have small people's bones instead of her own coarse, heavy ones. She'd have preferred to fit through all the doorways.

We felt sorry for Miss Stevens. Whenever she came over, we tried to make her part of things by intentionally standing far away from her, because in our minds it was less notice-able that way how little we were. Our mother and father made sure that Miss Stevens quickly took off her big coat and sat down on the lowest chair in the house. We talked a blue streak and all at the same time and pointed at all the low corners in the room and showed her four drawings at the same time, and we did all this standing up, just to avoid making Miss Stevens feel like a giant.

She would blush up to her hair roots, and her eyes would search out ours, as if at every moment she wanted to be sure we weren't kidding. She got this much attention only from us, and you could tell that it gave her heart palpitations. For a long time we thought that Miss Stevens had spells when she couldn't speak right, because she sometimes uttered half words or whole sounds. But later we discovered that it was our fault. A lot of the time we didn't let her finish what she was saying when she did try to say something.

My brothers and I couldn't help giving in to our enthusiasm. Since we'd heard from our mother that Miss Stevens was an orphan and that here on earth she only had God, we had become very attached to her. Of all the grownups who came to visit, she was one of the few for whom we stayed downstairs. We might not have heard any of the tall tales from her own lips, but we knew from our parents that Miss Stevens had seen Africa and had once been in a two-seater plane there and that she was sometimes bothered by homesickness but was never lonely, because a person who knows God is never lonely.

We didn't believe that God was enough for Miss Stevens. Lots of times we would build a complete farm at her feet. We'd all move around it on our hands and knees and milk cows, shear sheep, harvest beets, and ask one another questions we knew we couldn't answer.

"Do they have sheep in Africa?" we'd ask one brother, for instance, or "Does a cow moo the same way everywhere in the world?"

My brothers and I would shrug our shoulders and also say in words, "I don't know, don't ask me, I haven't seen very much yet," giving Miss Stevens a hint.

She always got it. She would apologize to our father and mother, often even before they had been able to start in on an interesting conversation above the table, and allow herself to slip off her chair and onto the floor. It made the farm very full. It would take us a while to get used to so much of Miss Stevens at our height, but we did grin a lot when we stared at her. We really were very attached to her.

Her backside hung like a heavenly body over our farmlands while the front of her flew over our farm, cooing like a wood pigeon. She would make a grab for a cow or snatch up a sheep and moo the way all the cows in the world moo, and she said that goats were the African sheep, which we thought was a strange assertion.

We didn't ask any new questions. A fire would flare up in Miss Stevens. It would race as if through spruce branches to all her extremities, to her feet, to her fingers. She knew exactly how cows were milked and beets were harvested. She drove a tractor the way it's supposed to be driven, and came to pick up the hay my brothers and I had piled up with the right kind of putt-putting motor sound.

Sometimes a giggle would escape her, and then she would look at us and we would look back at her. We smiled, but we were still a little sad. Our glances would drift down to the little silver cross on the collar of Miss Stevens' gray cardigan. God isn't enough for her, we would think. I believe Miss Stevens knew that that was what we were thinking.

Afterward we never knew exactly how long we had played together. The fire in Miss Stevens always went out suddenly, the way fire dies in spruce branches. A cup of coffee would suddenly be getting cold on the table, or she'd suddenly want a bite of a cat's-tongue cookie from the bowl.

Our father always found this a good moment to say that he had heard a noise in the attic and didn't my brothers and I have to go up and see what had fallen over. Our mother would say, "Boomboomboom," meaning the noise in the attic, and she would add that on our way up, our hands could have a look in the cookie jar.

"Oh, you dear children," Miss Stevens would say at moments like that, and if we looked at her then, we always thought her smaller than she had been at first.

Our mother stored up smells. When she made a cross over us before we went to sleep and caressed our cheek with her forefinger, her hand reminded us of the day past. The smell of peeled onions clung to her hand, and the pot roast appeared on the table again. From the hint of floor wax, we remembered the way the house had smelled when we got home from school. The scent of the Spanish soap that she always got from the same neighbor lady, and thought was very nice in spite of that neighbor lady, made us recall that we had leaned against her for a long time in the kitchen that evening, but really not long enough.

By the time we had to go to bed and she was darning socks and watching TV, she had had a long time to store up the fragrance of flowers because the socks smelled of the washing machine and now her hands did too. Her fingers reassured us: nothing has changed.

"God bless you and keep you," she would say, and the little cross she made was as thin as her voice. She drew it carefully on our foreheads and made sure we would be able to retrace it long after bedtime because she knew that our foreheads had a memory that made us sleep better. We would curl up under our blankets the way pandas do and think of our mother's fragrances.

Once when I was almost asleep, a brother sat up in bed, switched on the bedside lamp, and said that our father always smelled of the same thing, of tobacco from the blue packet, and had we ever noticed.

"I know," said my other brother, covering his eyes with his hand, "that there are people who have no smell of their own, and they aren't the nicest people. Turn off the light."

"And you can sleep?" asked my one brother.

I stayed curled up under my blanket with my eyes shut. I thought about what I already knew. I knew that some graves had no smell, and there was also something about the dead who had risen, but the idea that our father sucked blood or had been dead before I didn't want to investigate. I went over it quickly. Had our father ever smelled of anything other than the tobacco from the blue packet? I wanted to know that quickly, and in my mind I was sitting next to him last Sunday, leaning against him, and this summer I was sitting on his shoulders with my hands on his cheeks. And when was it that I had fallen against his leather vest and had had to laugh really hard so I'd stayed close to him longer?

When I had finished laughing in my mind, I couldn't laugh in reality. I sat up in bed and stared at my brother.

"As far as I know, Dad doesn't smell of himself," I said. "To start with, he smells of tobacco, and sometimes the leather of his vest, too, and pomade, Roya pomade, the best and the finest, the way the ad goes."

"Yes," said my brother. "That's right. So?"

So, nothing. That was the answer to his question, no matter how unsettling. It was possible that our father had no smell of his own. It wasn't a problem for me to check this out for my brother, but after that he would have to go to sleep, because I for one was getting very upset by all of this.

"Where are you going?" asked my brother.

"To smell," I said, and I went downstairs, where our father and mother were still watching TV.

When I came in, my father snapped his fingers, hard, for me to be quiet, the way only he can. I walked over to him on my tiptoes, and I leaned against him, heard his chest wheeze, and said I hadn't received a cross from him.

"You didn't?" he asked, and he had to laugh, and laughing made him sneeze, not once but three times, hard, and the force of it caused another one of his gates to open, which our mother said wasn't nice.

Then he gave me a little cross. As always, his cross wasn't a cross. He made it with a sloppy brushstroke so that it seemed more like a loop, almost a little circle that he placed on my forehead as he held my head still with his other fingers. As always, I heard the rubbing of his thumb on the inside of my skull as well.

"God bless you and keep you."

"So?" asked my brother when I crawled back into bed.

"I think," I said, "that our mother stores the right smells and our father stores the noise. And don't worry, he also has a smell of his own."

SWIMMING POOL

My brother and I dove into the water and swam a few strokes. The world looked very quiet and very blue. We felt so peaceful that we even started smiling and humming, but when we came up, the rest of the world, much to our surprise, was all astir.

My other brothers, who moments before had lain sprawled on their towels, had jumped to their feet and were trying to gather up their clothes. They bumped into one another, leapt hither and thither, and softly urged, "Hurry! Hurry!" They meant that we had to get out of the water and make sure we got away, and that there wasn't any time to dry off.

My brother and I were quick—very quick, to say the least. I even think my brother leapt straight out of the water, which may seem likely, although it's not—jumping from the deep end onto dry ground just like that—and yet he did it as I watched. After that he pulled me onto the side by my arms and dragged me into the bushes. This time it was a man who was after us. He bombarded us with the nastiest of words, but when they didn't seem to reach us, he started using clods of dirt and stones. My brother and I were quick, but not as quick as clods of dirt and stones. My brother got one on the head and shouted to my other brothers that they didn't have to wait for him, that he would just go and die for us. "Jump! Just jump!"

The seven of us jumped through the bay laurel and landed on the street. We were all still alive. Our bare skin was covered with scrapes and little insects, our hair was in tufts, and my one brother's ear was bleeding, making him even more of a hero than he already was.

"If I ever see even one in my swimming pool again, I'll hold him under!" shouted the man behind the laurel bushes.

At first we were frightened by the threat, but then we looked at one another and, as if by unspoken agreement, stuck out our tongues and made noises as if we had gas. That got the point across. We wanted the man with the swimming pool to know that murderers didn't scare us. We could hear him sound the retreat, panting and cursing. He shouted that he knew our names but that he didn't need to remember them, we'd show up in the papers soon enough with our hooligan mugs, trash that we were.

My brothers and I were quiet for a few seconds, but then we had to laugh. We had to laugh harder and harder. We doubled over, leaning on one another, and couldn't get dressed properly. We stuck our arms in our pant legs by accident and put our shirts on backwards, which made us laugh even harder.

We shouted back and forth that we had to stop, that we couldn't take any more, that we couldn't hold it anymore. Finally we all stood pinching our hoses with our thumbs and forefingers, because we literally couldn't hold it anymore. When we realized this about one another, we quieted down.

We looked at one another. Worse, we looked at one another with serious expressions and wondered what was really so hooligan-like about our faces. What was really so trashy about swimming in a swimming pool that never got used, in the back of a yard where nobody ever went? We didn't see any harm in what we had done.

My one brother said he had this feeling inside like a dog that had been chased away. He scared us a little saying that. He said dogs that got chased away knew instinctively that they had to take sweet revenge.

"Sweet revenge means quiet revenge," said my brother. "The person who chased the dog away will never know how the dog that got chased has taken his revenge."

We all nodded because we suddenly understood what my brother meant. We panted for a while like dogs, then pinched our crotches harder and followed at my brother's heels. He dove back into the bay laurel and walked zigzag, the way dogs do, through the bushes. We could already smell the blueness of the swimming pool. We were as quiet as could be, because the person who chased the dog away is not supposed to know how the dog that got chased takes his revenge. Sweet revenge is quiet revenge.

We took off our shirts. We quietly slid our shoes off our feet. We quietly stepped out of our pants and quietly pulled on our swimming trunks. The swimming pool was still rippling ever so slightly from what had happened just moments before, but the water thought that what we were doing was fine. It didn't make any noise when we slipped into it and stood in a row.

We waited for the signal from my brother. It was hard, with so much water all around us, but we held on. Only when my brother gave an emphatic nod did we raise our hands and give in. Yellow clouds grew around us. We looked at them and grinned and drooled a little, too, from all that sweet revenge. We even thought of diving under and enjoying the world down below, but we didn't.

We saved our joy for the swimming pool downtown. When we couldn't find a way to get in free, we bought tickets and played in the water like young pups. All seven of us hummed underwater with satisfaction. We hummed so hard you could hear it above the water.

INVENTIONS

My brother pointed at the wheels of his bicycle and said to my other brothers and me that we urgently had to amount to something meaningful. In all our lives, we hadn't achieved anything yet, he said, nothing that people would remember if we died tomorrow. He knew someone who at our age was already playing tunes on a harpsichord, and he had also heard of a boy of just twelve who had done a painting on a cigar box and had later become famous. Could we make a claim like that?

No, we couldn't. Songs we made up we had to sing because we couldn't play an instrument, and with paint we could paint but not do paintings. There was nothing we were strikingly good at or that we could get better at with practice. We had never yet discovered anything, nor had we ever invented anything yet. I remembered that we had taken baby carriages apart several times as well as an old washing machine and then a broken radio, too, but we hadn't succeeded in putting together anything of consequence with the loose parts.

My brother pointed at the wheels of his bicycle and said that we had to invent something important like the wheel. Something as useful as fire, the water faucet, or the incandescent bulb. Only then would we amount to something.

"It can't be that hard," said another brother. "It's a trick. You just have to try to think about things that don't exist yet. I won't say it's easy, but it's worth a try."

My brothers were full of confidence and lay down in the grass beside their bicycles. They looked at one another and particularly at my one brother, so that after a while they were all lying on their backs with their legs stretched out full-length and their arms under their heads, because that was evidently the best position in which to invent something.

I lay down too.

"Is this going to take long?" I asked.

"That depends," said my brothers.

It was quiet for a few minutes. My brothers lay staring at the clouds that floated pretty low over us. Their mouths were set in a serious way, and by their foreheads I could tell that they were thinking. With the sky above them, they of course first invented flying craft and a few things that needed wind. I saw it by the way they pursed their lips and moved their cheeks. On further reflection, they had to admit to themselves that they had invented a kind of helicopter and that anything that is "a kind of" has unfortunately already been invented.

My one brother said we had to stay closer to the ground and had better think of something small.

"You're right," said my other brothers. "It won't be any easier, but you're right."

I looked at my watch because I wanted to keep on bicycling and was slowly getting impatient, but because of the second hand I suddenly had to think about what my brother had just said and what my other brothers had replied—that it didn't get any easier if you had to think of something small. I didn't understand why my brothers were making it so complicated.

They lay spread out in the grass, moaning and groaning and feverishly looking for something that still didn't exist. Now and then a brother would slap his forehead or say "No, no, no" out loud. I felt their mood change, since they were getting angry with themselves because they had already been thinking for so long and still didn't amount to anything, while in my opinion inventions were there for the choosing.

I looked to the side and immediately knew that I, for instance, had to invent something with grass because that's what I was lying in. I also thought of something with ants because one was crawling on my arm, and I also had to invent something with smells because there were cows nearby, and something with little sounds that weren't noticeable, like the pounding of a heart or the scraping of a beetle's wings, and I felt myself becoming happy because of everything that gave me ideas for inventions. I thought of something with blackberries, because I wanted something like that, and I also knew that I had to invent something or other for the bottoms of my feet, because they kept itching more and more, and I also saw something with feathers before me, because I was getting so lightheaded, and then I dreamed I invented something that made a person smile, and to my surprise that invention was taller than the trees and larger than the meadow and woods around it.

My brothers sat up. They had only invented something small, like the curse and the sigh, and they weren't satisfied with that. They berated my brother.

"We're going to bike around for a while," they said. "You can go ahead and invent something like the wheel, and you can tell us all about it when we get back. Or go play the harpsichord or paint a cigar box, for all we care."

"I didn't say that we had to amount to something this afternoon," my brother kind of mumbled. "It can be tomorrow or next week."

My brothers got on their bikes and pedaled off, their heads between their hunched shoulders and the corners of their mouths turned down. I biked after them and after a while out in front of them. I was the only one who was looking around and discovering all kinds of things, whistling a tune all the while.

THE KING STOPPED BY

The king had stopped by. He hadn't been able to stay long because the queen was waiting in the car, but I was to have many greetings from His Majesty and he wished me many happy returns.

"Did he sing for me, then?" I asked, sitting up in bed.

"Uh—yes," said my brothers.

"Uh—no," said our father.

"Uh—yes, no, not really," said our mother. "He didn't have time or he would have sung."

"In French," said my one brother. "Because he does that the best. You can tell by his accent."

They promptly started singing for me in French, my brothers and our mother and father. They tried to sound like the king and stood closer around my bed, leaning forward and making me a little claustrophobic.

"Happy birthday!" they finally cried, but with the king's accent, and while they were cheering, they plucked me from my mattress and threw me up in the air, again and again and again, seven times. I was only too happy that I wasn't turning eight.

After that they let me catch my breath.

By the time I had collected myself, it finally dawned on me that the king had stopped by our house.

"Incredible," I said.

"Yes, incredible," said my brothers, the way the king would say it.

"And did he see me?"

"Yes, of course," said our father. "And he was very pleased. He said so himself, here in this house. 'I am incredibly proud'"—and this last he said the way the king would say it.

My brothers and our mother smiled broadly, and they said that the king had absolutely wanted to let me sleep, because he'd seen that I was busy growing.

"We are proud that he's your godfather," said my brothers, and they stared at me in a slightly glassy-eyed way as if they were covering something up, something that was green and resembled jealousy. My brothers' eyes slid to their corners, toward the foot of the bed, where our mother and father were standing.

"Is something wrong?" I asked.

"Yes," said my brothers.

"This," said our father. And he brought his hand forward from behind his back and held out a little chest covered with leather. It had a little golden latch and had come from the king. They didn't even have to say it.

"From him," I said, and I placed the little chest on my lap.

"You're old enough for his gift now," said our mother. "You can put it in your own closet. It's all yours, from His Royal Highness, specially for you."

A sigh passed through my brothers. They drew their heads down between their shoulders, but when I opened the little chest and couldn't help oohing and aahing, they stretched their necks again and oohed and aahed along with me.

"Incredible," they said, the way the king would say it.

His Majesty had given me something out of his own closet. In the little chest, on a pillow of white satin, lay a silver baby spoon and a silver goblet that was gold inside, and in the spoon and the goblet the first letter of the king's name was engraved, with a crown above it.

"Ooh!" I said.

"You can say that again," said my brothers. "That right there is a piece of the palace. The king had the first letter of your name engraved in that silver specially for you. See what a beautiful, curly letter? And see that? It has a little crown above it; he's just about making you a prince."

"Tut, tut," said our mother. "You're exaggerating."

"Well, didn't the king say that?" said my brothers as they winked far too noticeably at our father and mother.

"Well, no, he didn't say that," said our father.

"OK, we're lying," said my brothers.

"You're all incredible liars," I said, but I did have to laugh because I accidentally said it the way the king would. After that, I questioned them about what he had been wearing and whether he had said anything about me and whether the queen, growing impatient in the car, hadn't started honking.

ROBBERY

The best ambush is the almost impossible one. If the soil stinks, if the bush pricks and has branches growing thickly, close to the ground, if, on the way there, little twigs and leaves have already crept under your clothes, if you aren't sneaking but wriggling, if you think you can't go back any more, you've chosen a good spot.

"Now me," said my brother.

I lay beside him on my back and stiffened in fright. Above me in the bush hung an old nest. You could have asked me how a young blackbird would have felt if he'd flipped over the edge and been lying there waiting for a cat.

"This is going to end badly," I said.

"Badly? No, it's not," said my brother. "In the worst case it'll come to an end. I sprint up the street, I stop the van, I ask if he's got an extra loaf of bread, and before I've finished my sentence, you all will have grabbed an apple pie."

"And you really think he won't see that?" I asked.

"Oh, be quiet," said my brother. "He doesn't like small talk, he's always in a hurry. His bread's got to be ordered and fresh dough has to be put in the oven too. Besides, the sun will be shining in his mirror."

"This is going to work," said my other brother. "One: a good ambush; two: a good plan; and three: soon we'll be eating apple pie."

He fell silent. In the distance we could hear the little bakery van. It stopped and started up, stopped and started up. Each time only one door slammed, because the baker left the doors at the back open. That was easier. The loaves, some still warm, were stacked to the left, the pies to the right. Behind the little vehicle there was always a banner of fragrance. You almost wanted to take a bite out of the air.

My one brother was getting nervous. He tried to stand up inside the bush and wriggled through the branches.

"Do your best," my other brothers said to him. "Get ready."

"You too," said my brother. "Be quick."

The van rounded the corner. The baker put on the brakes when he pulled even with the vet's house, left the engine running, shouted something to the vet's wife, and slammed the door of the cab.

"Get ready!" said my brother. "Here he comes."

The fidgeting in the shrubbery must have been noticeable from the street. It was impossible for it not to be. My brothers squatted and mustered their courage.

"Soon we'll be eating apple pie. Apple pie," they whispered, and they packed themselves closer together, ready to shoot off like an arrow and snatch the apple pie on their way.

I looked at the nest again and shut my eyes.

This is going to end badly, this is going to end badly, I thought. I heard the delivery van drive away from the vet's house. It was as if he were driving from one side of my head to the other, across my racing heart.

"Now!" my brothers hissed.

"OK," said my brother, and he leapt out onto the street, and at just about the same moment the brakes of the delivery van screeched. The sound was brief, but hard and high.

We knew right away that our brother would have no time to start a question, let alone call out something.

The baker wouldn't have understood it anyway. From the shock, his body first lurched forward, then back. The loaves of bread copied him. They lurched forward, then back, the pies, too, in one sliding motion down the street.

"This will, uh ... end," said my brother.

"End," said my other brothers, and then we noticed the disadvantages of the best ambushes. And all along I had wanted to tell them about that old nest.

BEING GOOD

Because we all sat together in a bunch and nothing about us changed, passers-by asked what we were doing. We said we were bored. That was a good answer. It made people continue on their way. That was how we wanted it.

When yet another person had given us a friendly smile and even winked, my brother waited a moment and then asked us if we'd seen it, the problem, if we'd seen it.

"Can hooligans be talked to?" he asked as he looked at us one by one. "Would anybody dream of asking some punk what he's doing or what he's planning to do, wink, wink?"

"No," we replied in a single voice. "Nothing bothers punks."

Because we said this in unison, it instantly became clear. We were being good. We had a good name. Everybody knew everything about us: who cut our hair, that the shorts we wore used to be trousers. Everybody knew that my brother had a mole on the calf of his leg, and it was common knowledge that for years now there had been a dent in my other brother's back. Lots of people had already seen the dent. We had no secrets.

"This has got to stop," said the brother about whom everybody knew that he had once tried to juggle a mop and a rag and that it hadn't worked out right. The healing of the hole in my brother's head afterward hadn't worked out right either. That he had started squealing like a pig, this should also have stayed in the family, but you can't always button up somebody else's lip, so the story about the pig was told and retold for years until everybody knew it, and their children did too, and their great-grandchildren, so to speak.

"Stop, *basta*," we said, as if from then on we would make mincemeat of everybody and everything, even our words.

"Stop, *basta*," said my brother, who was known as the boy who sang in the choir but really never sang, really just moved his mouth, the whole church knew that. "We'll be, uh ... ruthless!"

"Ruthless?" I asked.

"That's right," said my brother. "People will see the difference. They may think they know everything about us, but because of our new behavior they won't ask what we're doing, wink, wink, anymore." He stood up, looked down at us, and stuck his finger in the air for us to listen to him.

As if my brothers and I had arranged it, we started to mutter and stew—this went with the new behavior. No, we were not going to listen to him, who did he think he was? Sit down, man, sit down.

"Sit down," said my one brother, who could fold his ear scallops into his ears and was often asked to do this. "And shut your trap." He made the longest face he could, made his eyes darken, and acted as if my brother who was standing up wasn't there. He asked us what we thought of kids, little kids, the littlest kids, really. Wasn't it better to dig them under so they could grow? Shouldn't they get knocked around more? Weren't you supposed to go find them milk or a crust of bread to build up their muscles?

"Aw, shut up," my brother who was standing up said suddenly. "You acquainted with my fist yet? Wanna get knocked into the thistles?"

We muttered and stewed again. We thought we were doing very well. We also discovered that it looked really bad if we kind of scowled from under our eyebrows and punched one another in the head.

The church clock showed that it was dinnertime, but we made no motions to leave. We kept on sitting there behind the thistle patch and waited for our mother to call us.

When she called us, we nestled our rear ends even more deeply in the grass. To hell with dinner, we said to one another, punch, punch, our mother could go and eat that stupid food herself, punch. We tried not to giggle too much because punks don't giggle all the time, but it was hard to suppress.

The passers-by saw what they were supposed to see. They read on our faces that, just like looters and murderers, we were enjoying our worst side. If it went on like this, nobody would ever ask us again, wink, wink, what we were doing.

"Time to eat!" our mother called once more.

"Pancakes," one passer-by informed us. "It's Saturday."

We fell silent.

"Mm," we all said at the same time. Nicely.

He was right; it was pancakes, the way it was every Saturday at our house. Everybody knew that, and their children did too, and their great-grandchildren, so to speak.

SWARM

One moment we were still talking about the clobbering we were going to give them—whether they could expect one right in the face or from the side, on the chin. We described what they would look like after that, the stupid jerks, and we acted out how they'd be standing there all bent double, the look in their eyes.

The next moment we forgot all about them.

From behind the trees a cloud was fast approaching. My one brother saw it first. He raised his arm and said, "Ho-ly smokes!" We followed the direction of his finger and then cursed as well. The cloud was made up of birds. We had never seen so many all together before. There were hundreds of them. They moved through the air like a swarm of bees, from one side of the sky to the other, and they twittered excitedly. It almost sounded like being laughed at.

"Those are starlings," said my one brother, because a couple of brothers were talking about sparrows, and he said that we couldn't compare this to anything else, not to a swarm of bees because bees were smaller and flew differently, and no, not to a cloud, not even a moving one, because a cloud was white and didn't change shape so quickly, again and again.

"They're playing with the trees," said my brother. "Look."

Sure enough. One of the starlings was tired and wanted to sit down. It flew over to a poplar tree, and because of that, all the other starlings hit on the same idea, you could tell. They swarmed into the tree, and because there wasn't any more room in the one tree, they decided to take over another one too. They sat there for a while, twittering, about the view, about their future, and who knows, about us in the distance, but not one starling finished its conversation because all of a sudden the nastiest piece of impatience got it into its head to fly to the other side of the sky again, and the whole swarm copied it, until another starling got tired and sought out a tree.

"It's a miracle," said my brother.

"Yes, a miracle," said my other brother. "But anyway, we were talking about the clobbering we were going to give them."

"The clobbering," we said, and we walked with our eyes trained on the other side of the little stretch of ground we were next to. We weren't allowed to walk on it because the farmer became outraged over trampled grass. We looked over at the honeysuckle with the hut under it. We assumed there was a hut because the biggest hole in the bush could well be a door.

"There are three of them," said my one brother, and he nodded at the boys who were crawling in with stuff under their arms and coming back out without the stuff.

"I think they're going to paper the walls," said my other brother.

"That's ridiculous," we said.

We didn't know the boys. They had a name that we usually pronounced in such a way that it sounded like spitting, and only my oldest brother had talked with them once, but it hadn't lasted long and had also seemed more like a string of expletives than a real conversation. They were known for their lack of manners.

The stories about them that made the rounds were tall tales. Some stories, like the one about the dachshund in the gutter, were heroic, and we would recount them as if we had been there. But most of what was said about the boys was about fire and glass and light fingers, so then we were saints in comparison.

"Which clothesline did they get those sheets from?" asked my one brother.

"They'll steal anything that's not nailed down," said my other brother.

"They deserve a beating," we said.

We stood up, slapped dirt and dry grass off our pants, and balled our fists in the direction of the honeysuckle. Come on, we thought. Come on! We almost started shouting at the other side, the ugliest words lay ready on the tips of our tongues, but we held them back.

The starlings flew overhead. We felt the wind coming out from under hundreds of wings. They stirred the air above us into a commotion, and their shadow flattened the grass.

"Better look out," said my brothers. "Soon enough they'll have eaten cherries, way too many cherries, and then all kinds of things'll fall out of the sky, and it won't be pits or beans either. Man oh man, too bad it's not money."

We roared with laughter, particularly because my one brother said starlings weren't donkeys. We spluttered with laughter, slapped our thighs, and pointed at the donkeys we saw flying around and pointed at the honeysuckle we saw on the other side, the way the hut was being buried under filth.

All of a sudden we forgot to laugh. We heard expletives. We didn't know what came over us. The stupid jerks were making their way across the little stretch of ground toward us through the tall grass, swinging their arms. They showed us with their hands what was going to happen to our necks, and they were already discussing what color our faces would be and how far our tongues would loll out of our mouths.

My brothers and I looked at one another. What had we done?

"Jealous!" they cried. "Jealous!"

"Jealous?" we said when they were standing tall in front of us.

"Yes, jealous," said one of the stupid jerks. "You think we didn't see you looking at us?"

"Ha!" said my one brother, and he made a sound with his tongue. "We weren't looking at you at all."

"Oh no?" the three stupid jerks said at the same time. They weren't afraid of being clobbered. They imitated the sound of my brother's tongue and said that they didn't appreciate our spying on them, that we should go build our own hut.

"Heck, no," said my one brother, and made the sound with his tongue again, in exactly the same way. "We only look at things that matter."

My brothers and I started snickering, which sort of came down to a clobbering, particularly because our snickering was reinforced by the laughter of hundreds of starlings. They were fast approaching over the cherry trees, and they had eaten cherries.

PUNISHMENT

In the summertime, we lived above a little grocery store that had everything. The store made it easy for our mother because she didn't have to go far for groceries. But our parents didn't realize that they were asking the fox to mind the henhouse. For us, it was torture living for two months above the closest candy bins in the country, on top of all that sweetness and fragrance, and being allowed to touch it only with our eyes.

"Anybody who gets caught is going to get it," said our mother when the vacation was barely an hour under way.

The first week we went out scouting in the east and the west. On one side lay dunes as far as we could walk, and on the other stood large houses in which people who wore golf clothes lived. The sea lay to the north, and we weren't allowed to go south—that was the other side of the coast road, and according to our mother, a child was run over by the tram every summer, and it would be very inconvenient if one of us became a newspaper headline.

"Anybody I see on the other side is going to get it," she said.

On the map in our minds, the grocery store was in the middle and the rest lay around it. We felt at home.

After a week, the Baeckes were unexpectedly left with us. We looked at them as if they were dogs that had been kicked out of the car en route. There was no room for them. My brothers and I had also already drawn a map of ourselves, with my one brother in the middle and the rest of us around him.

"There are rules," said our mother to the Baeckes. "Anybody who doesn't stick to them ..."

"Is going to get it," we said in unison.

"That's right," said our mother, and she went down to get milk at the grocery store. She left us alone in the overly cramped room.

Gregory Baecke sighed. From his face we could tell that he thought there was nothing going on at our place. He preferred to be alone. He had a mouth that looked tough and eyes that sought adventure and usually found it, too, and if there was no adventure, he would find something else. From the very beginning we disliked him. We totally loathed Felicity Baecke. She was a girl.

"Don't think we like being saddled with you guys for two weeks," said my one brother.

"You took the words right out of my mouth," said Gregory.

We shuffled back and forth nervously and started looking around to see if there was a spot somewhere where my brother could fight it out with Gregory.

"Let's show a little respect," said my brother, while with his hand he mimicked a mouth that opened and shut. "Our Mr. Baecke has only just arrived."

"Let's show a little respect," said Gregory in the same way. "Mr. Baecke won't be staying long."

We groaned in the backs of our throats and started breathing differently from the excitement.

"OK, wrong way to start," said my brother. He looked around at us, nodded once, and said maybe we should try the friendly approach.

"Take it easy," he said. "Our mother will let you grab a handful of candy downstairs as long as you eat it on the other side of the coast road. That's the way she wants it."

The brother who was standing next to me had to laugh, but he acted as if he were sneezing.

Gregory placed his hands on his hips. He pointed at his sister with his chin and at the bag of crepe paper flowers she was holding.

"Be nice and friendly to her, too," he said. "Just tell us where the beach is. She needs the beach for her flower store. She was hoping you all would be happy with a girl for two weeks, but I already told her that nobody could be happy with a girl for two weeks, so you won't have any trouble with her. And the same goes for me."

Gregory pushed his sister aside and walked out of the room.

"Hey!" said my brothers and I. We scrambled down the stairs behind him. "Where are you going?" we asked.

"To scout around," he said.

"Oh, OK," we whispered. "Don't forget the candy."

"No," said Gregory.

Thonk! went the bin of chocolate bars when he took off the lid. Our mother, who was over by the dairy products, heard it as well. We saw her jaw drop. We saw her eyes grow large when Gregory crossed the coast road without batting an eye and sat down on the other side to eat the candy.

We went downstairs and over a little way to lie on top of a dune from where we had a good view of the other side. It wasn't long before our mother came out, crossed the coast road, and showed Gregory that there was a lot going on at our place.

Our father took my hand, looked inside, and had to sit down. He couldn't believe his eyes, he said. They were playing tricks. Had I really found one?

I made a fist. The shell was inside, and it was mine.

"Come here," he said. "Confession time." He pulled me onto his lap to hear me out. Hadn't I made that thing in my hand myself? Had I by accident taken the shell out of the things belonging to another boy on the beach? And did I know what it was worth?

"It's a shell," I said.

"It's a shell," said our father. He shook his head, stuck his finger in the air, and repeated again what I had just said, only more slowly. He gave weight and polish to his words so that the shell became heavier and gained in significance.

His voice drew onlookers. My brothers, who had already been listening in with big ears and forgotten their scoops and shovels, came over and stood around our father and me, waiting in anticipation.

"I found a shell," I told them.

"Let's see it," they said.

"Let you see it?" said our father. He laughed and made

sure that he lowered his voice so it scared us a little. On the beach, life just kept on going. Children built sand castles, mothers sunned themselves, and kites flapped in the wind, but here, in my fist, suspended between my brothers and our father, lay a shell of significance.

"Hardly ever," said our father. "As good as never. Seldom, to my knowledge. A shell like that is seldom found."

We were silent. We looked at our father. How often was hardly ever? How often did as good as never happen? What was seldom? As far as we knew, that was a new word in our father's mouth.

"What should I say," he said. "Maybe once in uh ... ten years a shell like that is found. Once in ten years. It's unbelievable that this has happened to us."

"To him," said my brothers, and they shook their heads and nodded at me.

I held my breath. My fist burned. Moments ago a shell had been inside it. Now it was a treasure.

"Come on, show us," my brothers insisted.

I stuck out my fist. My hand was a treasure chest.

"Look," I said.

My brothers leaned forward.

On the mounds of my palm lay the shell. It was not an unusual color, and it wasn't terribly new, either, but there were little grooves in it as if something had bitten it, and it had a shape I had never seen before. A little cap it was, a knit cap that had once been pointed but now had been worn too often. And it was seldom found. As good as never.

I pulled the corners of my mouth down and sighed. There were wrinkles in my thoughts. Moments ago I wanted to show a shell—look, Dad, something from the sea—but suddenly the sun burned less hotly and the sea was farther away. I could only think of seldom and hardly ever, and that just now ten years had gone by—ten years in which no shell like this had been found. Around me, children built castles, mothers lay on their stomachs, and kites tumbled on the wind. Meanwhile, another ten years had started, during which a shell like this one would not be found.

I closed my hand, looked around at the spot where I had found it, and had to sit down.

"That's really something," said our father.

FAT MÈNE

When Fat Mène bicycled up, we dared bet our lives on it that when she was even with our house she would try to have another accident. She stood dangerously tall on her pedals and looked inside our house to catch a glimpse of us, since she had a soft spot for all of us. We could set our clock by when she would raise herself off the seat and when she would sit down again and miss the tree by a hair.

One time we stopped her. We lied, saying that one of us also had his eye on her. We weren't going to say who, only that he had been wondering for a long time already when she would go swimming with him.

"So, which one of you is it? Why doesn't he ask me himself?" inquired Fat Mène.

"Because we're men of action, not words," said my brothers.

That reply sounded good, but they delivered it in the wrong way. They stared at Fat Mène's breasts when they said it. Because I was the littlest one and still had a lot to learn—a whole lot, really—I paid attention to everything at the same time. I saw Fat Mène's breasts and my brothers' eyes and the way their tongues ran over their upper lips. I think Fat Mène caught on, too, because I received a pat on the head and one brother got a slap that was intended for my other brothers as well.

"You're all the same pigs," said Fat Mène. She tossed her long hair over her shoulders and biked off. She veered past the tree that she always missed by a hair.

My brothers recounted from experience that girls always had to make noises before they could be kissed. They call you a pig and the next day they ask if you want to go out with them, said my brothers. But I couldn't know that yet, I was too little for that—much too little, really, they said.

"Yes," I said happily. "Much too little."

A day later, Fat Mène came bicycling along as if nothing had happened. She first stood up tall on her pedals, as always, but when she saw us, she got off her bike. She said, "I'm going swimming on Friday, I think," and she looked at us one by one.

"That's a good idea," said my brothers.

Fat Mène did something she had never done before. She picked up her bike, turned on her heel, and biked back toward where she had come from. We watched her go and could do nothing but shake our heads.

"Hams, hams," said my brothers.

"You can say that again," I said, because Fat Mène's rear made you think of food.

The theme of the entire week was the swimming pool. My brothers recounted from experience that girls who eagerly wanted to be kissed were actually very dangerous. They'd start carrying on with you, drive you crazy with their bodies, and then shove your head underwater. But I couldn't know that yet, I had to live a little longer—a lot longer, really, they said.

But meanwhile they waved their hands around. They said they wouldn't be able to hold back and that they were allowed to look at everything, but obviously not at Fat Mène's breasts, because then things would go wrong.

When I asked why they had changed from pigs into weasels, my brothers all fell silent. They stared at me and sized me up with their eyes.

"Aren't you scared, then?" they asked.

"No," I said. "She didn't slap *me*. Just the opposite."

"That's true," said my brothers.

There was a long silence. My brothers exchanged glances, thought long and hard, and now and then whispered a word I didn't understand to see if they were all thinking the same thing.

"OK," they finally said. "We'll admit it. We're scared of her. She slaps us if we look at her. So, we won't look on Friday, we've already decided that. You'll be our eyes, and you'll tell us later what you saw, OK?"

"OK," I said, and I asked them what I'd get for it.

"The more details, the more nougat and sourballs," they said.

I was really looking forward to Friday. I always loved swimming anyway, especially if my brothers were around, and paying close attention to Fat Mène was something different for a change.

"Glad you're going along," our mother said to her before we left. She nodded in my direction and asked if Fat Mène would look after me a little. "Take him with you into the changing room and make sure he doesn't put his swimming trunks on backwards."

I looked at my brothers, all of whom had a dry mouth, and grinned at the thought of so many pieces of nougat and packets of sourballs.

STANDSTILL

"He's sweating," said my one brother. "He's not doing anything, but he's sweating anyway."

We nodded and bent over a little farther. The toad between the rocks looked up at us and shifted its front feet, but might as well not have for all the difference it made. With this creature, moving was really the same as sitting still.

"That sweat is grease," said my other brother.

"Pus coming out of its pimples," yet another one said.

"Isn't it just wet?" I asked.

"What do you mean, wet?" said my brothers. "Toads don't swim. Toads aren't frogs."

Our mother crossed the lawn. She was walking from the laundry room to the porch with a basket full of clean sheets. She tried to look at us while squinting into the sun.

"Shouldn't you all be doing something?" she called over to us. "I have some work for boys who are bored."

"We're not bored, Mother," we said. "We're busy doing all kinds of things."

"Yes, I can see that," said our mother. "There are all kinds of ideas bubbling up over there. Unbelievable how they're brewing. What a life, what a life." She said this as if she were watching the foam on a beer fizzle down.

My brothers and I looked at one another. We'd just been berated for being lazy—that was how we saw it—for being pimply toads that sweat but don't do much else. We growled in our throats.

"If she thinks we're not doing anything … ," said my one brother, bending down. Before we knew what he had in mind, he had already snapped back up. We hadn't expected that he could bend down so quickly. We also hadn't expected that he would grab hold of the toad, let alone snatch it up in a single motion. We glanced from his smooth, expressionless face to his hands and wondered what he was going to do with the creature. Maybe we should talk it over first. Maybe we should let our ideas bubble and brew.

My brother thought not. He narrowed his eyes half shut and said it might seem like we weren't doing anything but we were really very busy. He did a couple of wind-ups and then, in a wide arc, lobbed the toad in the direction of the porch. The creature landed on the tin roof like a glob, but not a big one. We heard a plop.

"Let's go take a look," said my brother.

We needed a couple of seconds to close our mouths.

"Yes, let's investigate," we said after a while. We cocked our ears, knitted our brows, turned our hands into visors over our eyes so that we could bear the bright light. We eyed the gutter to see if something up there was hopping up and down from the heat or maybe had splattered.

Our mother came out to stand in the doorway.

"What are you all standing there for?" she called out.

"We're not just standing here, Mother!" my brothers and I clamored.

"What are you waiting for?"

"Nothing, Mother, we're very busy."

"Busy doing nothing. Right," said our mother. "Waiting for a miracle or something else to happen."

Our lips were sealed.

Above our mother's head, maybe three feet to the left, we saw something move on the edge of the roof. If you didn't look closely, it was black like a blackbird, but we knew better. We kept looking. We wanted to see how the toad would crawl over the edge, flop forward, and fall off the roof.

Our mother noticed when it was too late. She saw something pass in front of her and looked surprised when she saw what lay on the ground. She slapped her hand over her mouth and pushed her head up. She looked as if she expected a cloud up there that the toad had fallen off of.

"What's the matter, Mother?" asked my one brother.

"Is something wrong?" we asked. "Is something wrong?"

We ran in the direction of the porch.

"No, no," was all our mother said, and she waved her hands dismissively.

We came to a standstill a few steps away from her.

"Oh, no!" we all exclaimed in surprise. We pointed at the toad that was lying on its back, exposing its burned belly.

"A toad!"

After that we fell silent and didn't move for a time. It seemed as if we weren't doing anything, but we were very busy.

MEMÉE

When our grandmother came to a standstill in the middle of the room one day, no longer knowing where she was on her way to, my one brother slowly turned around and looked at my other brothers and me one by one. He nodded and sucked in the corners of his mouth, after which he said over his shoulder to our grandmother that she was going upstairs. She was going to look for something in her odds and ends drawer, had she forgotten?

"Yes, that's it," she replied, as if of course she remembered, but we could tell from her back that she had scared herself.

"I was going to have a look to see if I had a little eraser for you, because you asked me if I did," she said.

"A pencil, Memée," said my brother.

"Yes, that's it," said Memée. "A pencil with an eraser on it."

We went upstairs with her. Halfway up the stairs, my brother stood still and held us back with both hands. He planted them in the air as if he were putting up a wall.

"It's gotten to that point," he said, checking to see that Memée wasn't listening. "You all may not have noticed anything, but I have. This is already the second time in just one week that she suddenly doesn't know where she's going anymore, even though she's on her way to very normal places in the house. Last time it was on her way to the front door and this time on her way to her odds and ends drawer."

My brothers and I looked at one another. We heard Memée in her room, rummaging in her nightstand, and we automatically got the smell of the little drawer in our nostrils so we knew even less what we were supposed to think, since it seemed that something in the world had changed because of the smell. We hadn't noticed anything special about Memée, nothing to worry about.

My one brother swept aside the wall he had put up between us and brought his finger to his ear. We listened along with him to our rummaging grandmother and nodded at what we heard, just as my brother was doing. Memée muttered above the clinking metal and the rattling buttons and pieces of wood. Now and then a curse fell into the drawer.

Only when my brother shrugged his shoulders and shifted his finger to his forehead did we realize that again something was wrong. Of course: the rattling pieces of wood were pencils—that was a safe bet. The odds and ends drawer was full of them. Everything Memée found in the house she picked up, and often it was shiny new pencils or chewed-up stumps as well as pencils with erasers on them.

"She's still looking," said my brother. "You see? It's begun." He heaved a deep sigh and wanted to continue up the stairs, but I held him back.

"What?" I asked. "What's begun?"

My brothers all looked at me in that glassy-eyed way they always had of making it clear to me that I was young, very young—too young, really.

"Just think about it," said my brother. "What does a train do when it approaches the station?"

"That's right," said my other brother. "What does an alarm clock do when its spring winds down?"

"Or a rocking chair, in the end," said the brother who was standing closest to me.

"Stop," all my brothers said in unison, and they didn't wait for me to say anything in response. They wormed their way past me and went up the stairs.

"Stop?" I called up after them, and I was just able to grab one brother by the waist of his pants, so that he too had to grab a brother and that brother another, so finally all of them had to stand still and look around at me.

"First you say that something has begun, and then when I ask what's begun, you say that something has stopped," I said as slowly as I could.

My brothers looked me up and down, which made them stronger, and nodded.

"Stopping has begun," they said.

At that moment our grandmother swore at her night-stand. We heard wood creak and after that something hit the floor with a bang.

We raced upstairs, burst into the room, and breathed a sigh of relief. The odds and ends drawer was leaning upside down against the bed. Memée was standing there with a broad grin in the middle of a little pile of rulers and pieces of paper and dice and children's scissors and pencils and paper clips and rubber bands.

"Easy, easy," she said. She raised her hand and said, "I found it."

Between her thumb and forefinger she was holding a pencil sharpener.

My brother let his shoulders droop, making it seem like he was caving in a little.

"Oh, good, Memée," he said softly.

"Just what you were looking for, right, brother?" said my other brothers.

"A pencil sharpener," said Memée.

She held on to her smile until the muscles in her face began to falter, and then she slowly let herself sag down on her bed.

PIT

Our mother asked if we already wanted to die. She had never posed that question before. We spread our arms a little so she could see that she had scared us. If she followed the direction of our hands, she would know that we didn't want to die, that on the contrary we were building our future. We had been in the dunes all afternoon. Before you could start putting a floor in a pit like ours, you had to figure on a few hours of digging. You didn't make that kind of pit with two rooms and a hallway in between just like that. Couldn't she see that all that time we had been good brothers who had worked together, without quibbling, to get nice, smooth walls, and now we just had to lay a nice, flat little floor?

"And what do you all think you're doing?" she asked from up top.

We shrugged and said, "Putting in a floor."

"Putting in a floor?" she asked.

"Yes, a floor," we said. "And after that we'll be done."

"After that we'll be done? After that we'll be dead!" she said, and she closed her hand around her neck and stuck out her tongue as if she had choked. "Get out right away. Now!"

We took a step in the direction of the little ladder leaning against the wall, but my brother held us back. He nodded at a growing pile of sand on the bottom of our pit. If you ran your gaze straight up from there, you ended at Felicity's forehead. We could have guessed that she was clinging to our mother the whole time, but we saw her only now. She had kept quiet. Tattletales always keep quiet and look triumphant.

"Out!" cried our mother. She meant it.

We climbed out of the pit one after another and grumbled under our breath. We held our shovel in such a way that we could bop Felicity into the pit the minute she said one wrong word.

"Glad you told me what they were doing, Felicity," said our mother. "A pit like that is more dangerous than the entire coast road and the coast tram put together." She laid her arm around Felicity's shoulders as if she had exchanged us for a daughter and said we had to fill in the danger pronto before it filled itself in with somebody inside.

"But Mother," we began, but our mother wanted to hear nothing besides yes and amen. She shook her head to avoid our pleading looks and even turned her back on us after a while, so she couldn't see us at all anymore.

We stuck our shovel into a pile of sand as if it weren't a pile of sand but a stomach or a behind and filled in our work for the day shovelful by shovelful. We cursed a little at our mother, although not very loudly because we loved her.

We didn't love Felicity, so we tore her limb from limb, left nothing of her whole. We thought of how we would make her pay for it, whom we would bribe, and how we could break the well-intentioned crepe paper flowers she always made, without anybody suspecting us.

By thinking of Felicity, we got the pit filled more quickly than we expected. Now and then a piece of wall would collapse, but then we acted as if we had meant for that to happen.

"OK, good," we'd say.

When we got home to eat supper, we tried to stay out of Felicity's way, but the table wasn't big enough. Our father sat at the head and asked what we'd done that day. Felicity smiled at him and said she had made flowers that she had sold right away, and this made our father nod his head.

"And you all?" he asked us.

We moved the tops of our bodies as if we couldn't decide what we should list first, and finally said that we had played in the dunes. We expected a comment from Felicity, but she didn't get the chance because our father asked, "And your brother, Felicity? Where is your brother? He's late for supper again."

"Gregory always forgets what time it is," said Felicity.

My brothers and I thought the same thing at the same time. As if we had arranged it, we looked up at the same instant. Gregory was late for supper. With a little bit of luck he would forget what time it was until after dark. That seemed long enough for us. We looked at Felicity and smiled at her in a friendly way. We simply repeated what she herself had said, that Gregory always forgot what time it was. Time. Gregory. Forgot.

"We dug a pit, Dad," said one brother suddenly. "And after that we filled it in again, because it was getting much too dangerous. It might have collapsed with somebody in it."

"With one of us in it or with Gregory in it," we said. After that we looked at Felicity again and grinned at her and waited patiently until she turned pale.

"Where is he, I wonder," said our mother helpfully.

THE ONLY WAY

My brother said there was no way back, but I thought that was strange because we had obviously come from some-where.

"Come on, get going," he said. "Don't look back because it won't help. The only way is the one in front of us."

I looked at the only way there was and at the back of my brother, who was keeping up the pace. He walked with a spring in his step, even though he was wearing boots that were too big for him, and he swung his arms as if he had joined the navy. My other brothers and I moved a lot less, even with our mouths. We clenched our teeth from the effort, and all our muscles were taut, because in between us hung a boat that had been somebody else's only an hour ago.

The inside was white and the outside was red, and my brothers were happier than I was. I just sensed this, but I knew it, too, because they'd put on other faces. An hour ago they had suddenly started behaving differently, as if they had turned into sailors and had gotten sturdy calf muscles that they had to shake all the time to loosen up. They also had to keep putting their hands on their hips and spitting on the ground. And then their voices had started sounding even louder, too, although there was no wind for them to yell over.

Now they were silent. Only my one brother who had his hands free and was walking in front of the boat sang "Hey" and "Ho" to make sure we kept up the pace.

I took two steps for every one and a half of theirs. At a certain point, I felt I had to say that the boat we had bought really wasn't a big boat, almost not a real boat, in fact. Because that was my opinion.

In front of, beside, and behind me everything suddenly began to pull and shove and bump. My one brother cried "Hey" three times in a row and then "Ho" a couple of times, raising his arms as he did so while turning in our direction. The boat was lowered to the ground in a single motion, rocked back and forth a little as if it were floating, and with a groan from everybody's lips, everything around me came to a standstill.

"Do you realize what you're saying?" said my one brother. "If this boat were a person, you would have really insulted it. Do you realize that? Do you realize what we got in exchange for our money? An Optimist with a keel and everything, with a sail and everything. Do you realize what that costs new, an Optimist like this with a keel and a sail and all?"

"Not a big boat," my brother sneered, mimicking me.

"Almost not a real one," said my other brother in the same way.

They all went *tss* at the same time to give me the feeling

that I still had a lot to learn, a whole lot, even—everything, really.

But I kept feeling what I felt. It's not because a boat has gotten a name that it suddenly gets bigger. An Optimist with a keel and a sail and all remains a little nothing of a boat, even if it's called an Optimist.

I didn't say it in so many words. I only asked who was going to be the first to get in, because in my view it could fit only one person at a time.

"The oldest, of course," said my one brother.

"Ask who'll be the last to get in, why don't you?" said my other brother as he pointed in my direction with his chin. They all had to laugh at that, as loudly as old deckhands, and they made coal shovels out of their hands with which they slapped one another on the shoulder.

"Come on," said my one brother, who, an hour before, was planning to become a whale hunter. "We have to keep going. Looking back doesn't help. The way to the canal is long, straight, and the only one."

My brothers nodded with their borrowed faces, and it struck me that they were even happier than a little while ago. It radiated from them. They were the proud owners of an immense boat in which they would sail the seven seas and maybe even discover the eighth.

I placed my hand on the part of the boat I had paid for and helped carry their dream. The entire only way I kept my mouth shut. What's more, I pressed my lips together. The entire length of the only way my brothers sang along to their feet. They sang "Hey" and they sang "Ho," and they were still singing when they lowered the boat into the water and saw the thing float with its keel and everything.

Then my one brother got in, and after that my other brother, and then a third, neatly according to age. They could tell I was right, but they didn't admit the boat was cramped. More cramped with every brother who got in. They kept maintaining that an Optimist was a big boat, a really real one, but when all my brothers were on board—the oldest, the quietest, the realest, the farthest, the nicest, and the fastest—they had to admit that there wasn't any room for me anymore.

I stood on the bank and watched the water wash over the side of the boat whenever anybody dared move. Then it seemed suddenly as if my brothers had sat down on a brick. Looking back wouldn't help because there was no way back. The only way there was, was down.

UNDER THE SEA

No time for cake, we had to go deep under the sea. We didn't understand how our mother could sit there and eat with a girlfriend she hadn't seen in a long time, while we—her own sons—bade farewell and went off to remove our clothes in the capsule that we called The Bathroom.

Behind our backs, we heard the girlfriend laugh. She sang a sailor's song about the sun setting in the sea.

My one brother sat down on the tall radiator so he could see everybody. He gave a speech about the importance of our assignment and said that we had to keep going, no matter how cramped it was down there. At the end of the journey, fortune would smile on us, we had to keep that in mind.

He glanced sideways to see whether anybody was still listening in, but the girlfriend we had never seen before, who also had no need to know that we were setting out on a dangerous journey, sat and whispered and giggled with our mother and had no interest in our adventure. They sang again, of the sea sunning in the sack.

My brother went aboard. He climbed over the high rim of the bathtub and disappeared underwater. Soon he was in the depths and motioned to us, what in God's name was keeping us? He couldn't hold his breath long.

My one brother was more daring than I. He shook my hand and with his other hand he tapped his forehead the way sailors do. He spoke perfect Russian and also bowed to our mother, who had come in to take a peek, and who, with a bottle of advocaat egg liqueur in her hand, wished us a safe voyage.

"Aren't you all in there yet?" she asked. We were later than usual, that was true. On account of our mother's friend, a number of things had ended up in a crunch. It was high time we were deep under the sea.

"The boys are leaving," our mother called over her shoulder. "It's almost time."

"Ahoy, ahoy," the girlfriend called back. "It's almost time."

My one brother climbed into the tub at the moment that my other brother spluttered to the surface.

"Come on," he said as he wiped the seaweed out of his face. "We have to go hunt." He stood up and started washing himself with soap so that he became clean and could get into his wetsuit. My other brother did the same thing.

By way of the washing machine, I climbed into the bathtub. There wasn't much room anymore. My brothers stood in the depths, foaming. I was able to stand where you were really supposed to sit, but I still had to hang overboard a little.

It was going to be a dangerous journey, I knew. Nearby, in the living room, our mother and her girlfriend sat and giggled, rocking back and forth. Maybe we had better stay home safe and sound, near the cake and the advocaat and the song they were singing.

"Have you scrubbed up already?" my one brother asked as he zipped up his own wetsuit. "Or aren't you going with us?"

"No, I am, I am," I said quickly, and I got the soap for about two seconds before they gave me a suit, quick-quick.

"Good," said my brother. "We can go," and he held up the piece of soap.

"We can go," said my other brother.

"We can go," I said, much too late.

The soap had already fallen.

My brothers dove after it. They risked their lives. It was all or nothing. If they found the treasure, fortune would smile on them.

They had been under the sea for only a couple of seconds when fortune came armed out of the living room.

The entire time, almost a whole minute, for as long as my brothers' rear ends stuck out above the water, our mother and the girlfriend we had never seen before stood near the bathtub, biting their lips. They pointed at the two backsides and made smothered sounds. Their cheeks turned red from waiting. They tried not to greet my brothers with smiles too soon, which was hard because they were very happy.

THE DARKNESS THERE

Our mother made the beds tightly on purpose so that it got good and dark under the covers. Black as death, certainly at the foot. The little bit of air was thick and warm there, and if I lay like a turtle with my legs drawn up and my arms folded under me, it got really stifling and impossible to bear.

When it was almost too late, when I had almost suffocated, when I was almost pissing in my pants from fear because I thought I would never reach fresh air in time, my brothers would come rescue me from the darkness. They would storm into the room, yelling, and jump on top of me, shoving and pulling one another and me until I appeared at the head of the bed like a baby out of a belly, gasping for air.

"He's still alive," some brother would always say, thereby explaining why I was smiling from ear to ear. My cheeks would be red and shiny from the heat and the heavenly glory. I would tingle all over, cheering inside, because I was still alive and my brothers were still alive, and I would hear Mother rummaging around in the kitchen, so she was still alive too.

Meanwhile, my brothers would storm out of the room,

rattling like machine guns and sometimes worse—roaring like bombs that exploded one right after the other, wreaking destruction at the top of the stairs and in the adjoining rooms. They would lie there, the six of them, motionlessly being dead, preferably with a chair knocked over on top of them, while I had to hold my stomach I'd be laughing so hard.

When our mother didn't have too much to do, she sometimes came upstairs, humming, to come to a standstill on the top step and convincingly take fright at seeing all those dead bodies.

She'd go "Oyoyoy," after which she'd throw her hands up around her head and wail that she was torn apart with grief, oyoyoy all my sons lost. But then she'd hear me giggling, and she'd pat her chest with relief.

"Still one who's alive," she would say.

She always fell for it. She was always good for a shriek when my brothers suddenly jumped up and shouted that they'd risen from the dead.

"Arisen," our mother would say, but she meant the same thing, and nothing could put a damper on the fun. We enjoyed the fact that we were still alive and let her know this by hugging her leg, but we'd also cling to one another or randomly pinch arms and legs because somebody who feels pain isn't dreaming.

But things didn't always go well. One evening in November, I was at the foot of the bed under the covers, curled up, anticipating the fun. They were to come rescue me from death, yelling as they usually did, just in time, just at the moment that I would reach the border between still and no longer. I listened to the muffled sounds around me and was startled to notice that my heart was panicking much more than usual. Soon it would miss a beat and burst, I was sure of it. I could hear it pounding in my ears, and now that I was all rolled up in a little ball, probably the way a butterfly sits in its cocoon, I could hear my blood pumping through my veins. It was stifling. I was suffocating. I broke out in a sweat that itched under my armpits, but I waited for my brothers as agreed. I started counting, not down, but up, although I didn't keep it up for long because when I noticed that the dark behind my eyelids was unusually dark, I lost any feeling I had for arithmetic. I didn't see lightning bolts, the way you always see them in the dark, and the now-and-then orange haze wasn't there either. Sounds from outside didn't come to me anymore. The only thing I heard were my own thoughts. I heard myself thinking that I was past the dark, for instance. Suddenly I knew: this is the darkness.

As fast as I could, as if I'd been stung by a bee, I wrestled myself backwards out from under the covers. I gasped for breath and opened my eyes, ready to grin in relief because I was still alive. But it remained dark, dark as death, and I had the horrible feeling that I had ended up alive on the other side of the dark, there where you're normally dead. I tried to call my brothers, but the darkness was also in my lungs, and their names got stuck in the back of my throat. There were snickering ghosts nearby. I could hear them. They even giggled. I thought a door was approaching me. Suddenly it was there. In the dark it was outlined with three strips of light, and it hummed like our mother. Then it opened up.

"I thought you were all dead," said our mother to the room, and she looked around in surprise at all my brothers, from the oldest to the fastest, who were everywhere, lying down or hanging, and who started roaring with laughter and wiping the tears from their eyes. They groaned, their stomachs hurt so much, as they pointed in my direction, they couldn't take anymore.

"No, no, we're still alive," they tried to say in one breath, but they couldn't manage.

"Why are you all sitting in the dark, then?" my mother asked.

My brothers would simply have to make up an answer to that question.

I became a turtle. I bowed my head and crawled back to the dark under the covers to die there, angry and miserable. Anybody who wanted to rescue me only had a few minutes.

PATIENCE

We saw Kummeling coming. He leaned heavily over his handlebars, a breaking wave on his bicycle. It took some effort for him to make it over the little bridge. Oh, the poor man, that Mr. Kummeling, our mother always said, because according to her he was bent up with rheumatism.

According to us he was crooked from drink. You could tell by his face and by the smell on his breath. He spoke in sentences without verbs, so nobody understood him, and was always scratching where it itched—under his cap or under his clothing, and at his neck whenever he thought about something. Kummeling was a man you preferred to avoid. You got a bad taste in your mouth whenever you saw him.

But he was lucky. He had a rabbit. Kummeling owned the only buck to be found for miles around, one that was known to do his work and be brought door to door as well. There was a rumor going around that the rabbit had a name that fit the animal. The rabbit was named Patience.

For use of the creature, Kummeling asked for a drink in return; two drinks was all right too. That was nothing compared to the litter that you got for it a month later.

As soon as Kummeling had waved to us from afar, we nudged one another, shouted for our mother to come, to come now with the drink, and went around the house to the area behind the garden shed where the swing set was, and the sandbox. Our father had put our hutch out there the week before, the hutch in which our Sunday dishes had been kept for years. Pitch had been smeared on top of it, its doors and drawers had been replaced by windows with chicken wire in front of them, and in the spot where the big casserole had stood was our new rabbit in clean straw.

"I think she knows," said my brother.

"She knows what's coming," said my other brother. "Look at the way she looks."

I didn't understand what he saw. There was nothing to be made of our Vera's expression. Her eyes were as round and brown and sweet as always. I didn't see any suspicion or expectation in them, and her nose didn't express any desire either.

She sat there eating clean straw.

Even when Kummeling came pedaling up on his bicycle, across the lawn, all the way to the back of the yard and under the swing set, she sat there. For a second, she perked up her ears and twitched them, because Kummeling cursed and barely avoided falling over, but for the rest she kept on chewing as if nothing had happened.

Only when a lot of movement suddenly started up in the basket that was tied fast to the baggage carrier with red twine did Vera hold her head still, and her mouth too. Her nose nervously went up and down, and her ears perked up and stayed that way.

We became uneasy for her. The wicker basket creaked noisily. It wasn't hard for us to guess that Kummeling's buck had nails that could break willow wickerwork, and we imagined that we could hear his jerking breath.

Our mother, who had come outside with a bottle of gin and a gin glass, asked if Kummeling was sure it was his buck he'd brought with him, because on the terrace just then she had thought of a lion, ha ha, he was making so much noise.

"Ha ha, a lion," we said, and we took a step back.

Kummeling flicked two wooden pegs out of a wicker ring, swung open the lid of the basket, and with one hand made a grab for his buck. He picked the animal up by the nape of its neck and held it up over his head.

"Patience!" he said.

Kummeling's rabbit didn't move, but you could see that his legs were strong and that he had big teeth he'd bite you with if you came too close to his head.

Kummeling was used to it. He opened our hutch, tossed his rabbit on the spot where the casserole had stood, and closed the door.

Then it happened as follows, and not differently. Kummeling accepted our mother's drink and didn't give her time to say you're welcome. We didn't have time to blink. Kummeling asked for a second glass, got a second glass, emptied it, and after that—and we are all sure of this—he had his rabbit dangling from his hand again.

My brothers claim that they saw what they needed to see. They saw something blunt and straightforward, something without verbs and a little like a breaking wave, like Kummeling himself.

"Too bad I missed it," I said to my brothers now and then during the month that followed. All of us would sit around Vera and try to comfort her and reassure her.

"Just a little longer, just a little longer," we'd tell her, and we imagined how the rabbits were growing inside of her with a little patience.

"We should have paid attention to the fire," my brother said in the dark. "We should have said: Just look, everybody, we're turning the fire off, we're turning it off with our left hand. See? It's going out."

He sighed. We hadn't paid attention to the fire. We had turned it off, we thought—we thought. Turned it off. But all the same it might be burning still, burning through the bottom of the kettle and burning out of the kitchen, burning the whole house down.

"Damn it," said my brothers in unison. "Just when the movie's starting."

"We can still leave," I said, but was startled by how small my voice was.

"Leave?" said my brothers. "How do you plan to leave? The door's locked."

I heard myself swallow.

"The door's locked," I said while looking over my shoulder. There wasn't a crack of light anywhere. You couldn't see a thing in the dark.

"It'll be a long time before the movie starts," said my brother.

Somewhere nearby somebody whispered that it would take even longer if we didn't shut up.

We were quiet. We thought of the kettle and of the hole that was burning in the middle of it and of the fire that would first lick at a towel, then at the jar with the wooden spoons.

We tried to listen to the music as it swelled and tried to concentrate on the first images, but in our heads the movie about the boys and the fire was playing. They stepped into their house through the front door, walked straight through to the kitchen, and leaned over the stove, all seven of them. The movie started with the words "You see?" Because the boys were shocked to see that the fire was still on, just as they had thought.

A voice said it was a stormy night, with wind and rain.

We could hear it, too, the wind and the rain. The theater was full of wind and rain.

"Oh, no," said my brother. "It'll blow out soon. If it's still on."

We could hardly understand him, but we knew what he was saying. We glanced at one another quickly and transmitted what we were thinking. The flame could blow out, if it was still going. Two guesses as to which is worse: a flame that blows out or a flame that spreads.

To my mind, blowing out was worse. In my mind, the flame had immediately gone out at the moment we'd shut the door and left for the movie theater. Soon our father and mother would come home. Who knows, maybe they wouldn't notice that it smelled of gas everywhere. They would take off their coats. They would put on their slippers. Our father would be in the mood to smoke his pipe.

"Where are my matches?"

I heard him ask. Our mother didn't.

"Where are my matches?" he asked.

"Don't do it," I said, and I covered my mouth with my hand and looked left and right beside me to see whether my brothers had heard me.

The brother sitting to my right shrugged and said, "It's only a movie."

On the screen, a man was being murdered in the wind and the rain, there was thunder and lightning, and there was enough noise for ten storms, but we were disturbing the audience. Somebody hissed in our direction.

"Shh!" It was probably on purpose that they made it sound like gas escaping.

We cringed. We squeezed our eyes shut from what we saw in our minds. The gas gained a head. The gas had a body that billowed out across the kitchen, the living room, the rest of the house. Silently it filled all the corners of the rooms, where it made itself invisible to our father and mother, who came home and didn't smell anything. They took off their coats. They put on their slippers. Our father was in the mood to smoke his pipe.

"Shall I put on some water for coffee?" our mother inquired.

"Oh, sure, coffee," said our father.

"What do you mean, coffee?" I said to myself.

I leaned over. "Brother," I whispered in the dark, "we didn't put a kettle on the fire at all. Our mother and father weren't at home, so nobody drank any coffee today."

"No?" asked my brother.

"No, now that you mention it," said my brothers. "We don't drink coffee. Coffee wouldn't have fit with the warm vegetable quiche that we only had to heat up."

"No," I said.

"Shh!" said somebody nearby.

"OK, shh," we said, and we sighed with relief. We motioned that we really would be quiet now and watch, but because the *shh* lingered on in our heads, it suddenly sounded as if we had taken the quiche out of the oven, but—had we turned off the oven?

It was quiet for a moment. Then my brother again said something in the dark.

"We should have paid attention to the fire," he said.

In the middle of the night there was a banging on the door. Our father heard it first. He sneaked down the stairs and called out, "Who's there?"

It was a man who wanted to be in our house. He babbled and bellowed at the front door; he slapped the flat of his hand on the wood.

"Who's there?" our father called out again, louder this time, because he wasn't planning to let in a man without a name.

My brothers and I knotted the belts of our bathrobes and sought shelter. We crept close to the stair railing, with a step or a brother at our back.

"Who's there? Hey! Who's there?" our father called out to the front door, his hand cupped around his mouth like a horn.

There was no reply. It grew quiet out in front of the door. We imagined that the drunk was standing there with his arms hanging down, reeling on the doorstep, and desperate—he would never get in. What was he supposed to do now, where was he supposed to go?

Above our heads, the roll-down shutters in front of the window of the little storage room went up. The window was opened, and an instant later we heard our mother call out.

She called out, "Yes?"

She didn't wait long for an answer. She slammed the window shut and arrived at the top of the stairs, shaking her head.

"It's Bert," she said, and added that he was mistaking our entry for his.

"How on earth?" said our father.

"Our entry for his," said our mother, and she gathered the lapels of her bathrobe and tiptoed past my brothers and me and our father on her way to the front door.

"Bert," she called out to the door. "Bert?"

There was movement on the other side. You could hear that Bert had four legs. And a thick tongue. He let loose a tirade. He said to the door that he wanted to come in. He had paid for the house and the planters and the venetian blinds and everything.

"Yes, OK," said our mother. "There aren't any here. They're farther down."

"They're here all right," said Bert. He wasn't some stranger off the street; she shouldn't try to tell him anything. He had paid off the whole house for her and the planters and everything, her ventian blinds, too.

"Venetian," we all said at the same time.

"Like I said," said Bert, and we heard him ramming his shoulder against the door.

Our mother took a step back. Our father sprang to life. In a minute, he'd ram his drunken head through it, he said. In a minute, he'd be lying flat on his face in the hallway.

"Bert," said our father, and he tried to explain to the door that Bert's house was farther down and that there were planters next to his entry. Big, expensive planters with dahlias in them.

That was too complicated for Bert, much too complicated. He cursed his wife and the kid and the house and that she was always thinking of herself and the kid and never once of him, her and her delalias.

"Dahlias," we said.

"Like I said," said Bert.

That's when our mother had had enough. She motioned to my brothers and me and drew us to her or pulled us up in front of her. She tugged at our collars and at our arms and held us close as if she were draping us around herself. After that, she asked our father to turn on the outside light and open the door.

"Oh. Sure," said our father, and he smiled. He did what she asked.

"So," said our mother to the outdoor air and to Bert.

"Like I said," said Bert, and he looked from our mother to my brothers and me. He steadied himself on the wall with one hand and rubbed his face with the other. He was really seeing double, he said. Really, really double.

"Number hunderd," he said.

"Hunderd seventy-eight," we said in unison.

BACK SEAT

By fitting and measuring, our father worked the baggage in. Everything that bulged he crammed, everything that was in the way he shoved aside, everything that was too lumpy stayed at home.

He slammed the lid shut and listened with one ear above the trunk to check if the pressure had caused something to break, but he heard nothing. His face brightened.

"Now, you all," he said.

"If there's room," we said.

We laughed nervously because not a single brother wanted to stay home. What's more, we were jumping up and down. We were going to the forests for the first time, and everything our father had said made them sound unusual. We would have a picnic at the highest point above sea level, and we would see where water came from.

We quickly crowded together, like suitcases of the same kind.

Our father opened the door and said, "Let's see."

One by one we climbed into the back seat. The oldest to start with, the farthest beside him, then another brother crosswise on top of them. Our father gave instructions as to how we could best place our legs or hold our arms, repeated that it would work, as if he wanted to convince himself, and gave us the example of the grown man who had crawled into a tiny crate and kept on laughing. It was a question of hypnosis.

"Hmph," we said.

The doors closed. Our father listened with one ear at the window to check if the pressure had caused something to break, but he heard nothing.

My brothers and I stared ahead. We secretly held our breath and pretended there was no problem. We were like the grown man in the tiny crate. If it had been up to us, we would have driven to the forests and back and up to the forests once again and only then picnicked at the highest point above sea level, and in driving by would also have taken a look at where water came from.

As soon as our father turned around, we let our breath out. We shoved one another, wormed a leg free here and an arm there. Now we could still shift and search; the car wasn't driving. We made our lungs smaller. We breathed out, we breathed in, we took turns breathing until we found a rhythm that felt good.

It was a question of hypnosis. This was how we'd get to the first of the forests. Maybe we'd even get to the highest point. Our bare legs were glued underneath and on top of other legs, our arms felt like they were braided, but we tolerated it for one another because we wanted to take a trip together, and if our father started asking himself questions, maybe the whole trip would be called off. What if he suddenly got it into his head that driving with such a full back seat wasn't safe?

"Anybody who lets out a peep will be dead tomorrow," said my one brother.

"Anybody who lets out a peep would have been better off being dead already," said my other brother. "We'd have gained some space."

We had to laugh, but tried to stop it right away because the shaking hurt, and there was little air in the car.

"Good-bye, house," said our father and mother as they got in.

"Good-bye, house," we cried, and as we drove away we tried to wave, but our elbows were stuck. At the first bend in the road, our entire body was stuck. We heard the way my one brother, who was sitting closest to the door, lost air.

"Everything OK back there?" our father inquired of the rearview mirror.

"Yes!" we cried. "Absolutely!"

Meanwhile, we were suffocating. We were sitting in a tiny crate. We entered bends and came out of bends, headed for the highway. Our breathing faltered. Our muscles strained. At the tips of our tongues lay the question if it was still far to the forests, the thought of a wide seat and lots of air playing through our heads. After a while, though, when we'd been on the highway for some time and no bend in the road had pushed us off balance, we noticed that it was really kind of cozy in the back seat. Our breathing had a rhythm. The asphalt had a rhythm. We brothers, we weren't often this close to one another. We even started humming, as if we were purring, and after a little while we thought up words to the song. We sang it softly, and from singing we forgot our sore arm or our leg that was stuck. It was a question of hypnosis.

"My foot's asleep," said my one brother suddenly.

"My foot too," said my other brother.

"It's working," I said. "Now the rest."

One day in August there was a man at the door. He had glistening hair and pink gums, and under his arm he had books in more colors than there are in a rainbow.

Did we want to be smarter, he asked. He asked twice, suddenly making it seem as if we were as dumb as boards, and deaf.

My brothers and I couldn't keep our eyes off the man. He glowed. He made your thoughts end up at a place where angels flew and a female choir sang.

"Yes?" our father suddenly inquired beside us.

The man's mouth opened. He showed his white teeth, and behind his eyes something began to glitter so that it seemed as if he had yet another face under the first one.

It confused us for a few seconds. We even had to gasp for air. My brothers and I nudged one another. We couldn't allow this man to keep standing there outside the front door. We certainly wanted to become smarter, since school would soon be starting up again. And if wisdom made you look like that man, we wanted to know the secret. We ran inside, left the door to the living room open, and made it clear to our father that the man deserved a chair. We all squeezed onto the sofa and in readiness cupped our hands behind our ears so we wouldn't miss a word.

Our father hesitated. "Uh, yes," he said as he let the man in. "What are you selling?"

"Uh, no," said the man as the room started shimmering a little because he was there. "What am I offering you."

"It comes down to the same thing," said our father.

"Not really," said the man. He rubbed the top of his forefinger and the top of his thumb together, let us hear how dry paper money rustled, and suddenly smiled so broadly that it became infectious. "Knowledge is priceless."

"Yes, priceless," said our father.

We felt the grins slip off our faces. You didn't get much for nothing. The books that the man had laid out in a fan on the coffee table cost a fortune apiece. We could see that at a single glance. There was a fortune lying there, times twenty.

"We're looking at it in the wrong way," said the man. "It's not about what knowledge costs, but about what it brings in return. Knowledge brings a lot in return. Knowledge brings joy."

He allowed his eyes to slide from left to right over the sofa, smiled at all of us, and returned his gaze to our father.

"Do we know everything?" he asked. "Do we know—I'll just pick something—how a Panama hat looks on our head, where the atlas is in our body, and where the Kurils lie? Do we know that?"

My brothers and I were shocked. We couldn't answer even

one question. We noticed right away that knowledge brings joy because we felt the opposite welling up. We looked at one another and at our father for help. We looked on our heads and in our bodies. We looked in the kitchen and went to the back of the yard in our thoughts, but we didn't find a Panama hat or an atlas, and where the Kurils lay, we also didn't know.

"Just by way of example," said the man, and he raised his hands. His life appeared much simpler than ours when he did this. That was obviously because of those books.

We could already see ourselves walking through the house, each with a volume under his arm, asking one another the most difficult questions. "I'll just look it up in Just Look It Up," we'd say, because that's what the books were called, and after a while we would start looking like the man, with his smile and his calm eyes and his face that never darkened, and we'd do very well at school. Everything now depended on our father, whether he wanted to know all kinds of things the way we did.

He did indeed. He looked at the man and he looked at us and posed exactly the right question to start off with.

"Where's my wallet?"

We knew the answer and let him know what knowledge brought. We jumped around our father with the wallet and cheerily sang out, "Just look it up," and finally draped ourselves all over him.

We understood. Our father had been through a war that was so terrible and lasted so endlessly long that it was talked about later only on Sundays or some other day when there was time. During our father's war, people were always wearing more clothes than now. In his stories, a bomb fell on the school, but after school, luckily; otherwise he'd have been dead. And across his fields tramped soldiers with mud on their boots.

We listened with open mouths and forgot what was getting cold on our plates. We were entranced by somebody who died for his homeland, and we didn't get scared when our father rattled and fell off his chair, because for us he was a soldier with mud on his boots and a bullet in his chest.

Because of the war, we understood why our father bought sprats now and then, or fatty tripe. The one was even worse than the other. But we understood.

For the sprats, he would start a fire in the fireplace, unroll the paper that was wrapped around the little sardines, and hold the tip of his tongue between his lips as he threaded the sprats one by one on a skewer. When the burning wood had changed into glowing embers, he would hang the skewer over them, and it wouldn't be long before fat dripped off the fish and little flames darted out of them.

Our father would bring his plate to the table and rub his stomach.

"A feast!" he would say. "The codfish of the poor!"

Fine, we thought, and we tried not to stare at him as he ate.

He ate as if it were wartime again. He would always enjoy his sprats with both hands, and his fingers and his chin would start gleaming from the fat. He would lick his lips and make smacking sounds the way we weren't supposed to.

For the fatty tripe, our father would heat up a pan of farmer's butter. The butcher would already have cut the innards into pieces. Every time, though, we thought he'd forgotten to clean them, because as soon as the pieces of fatty tripe landed in the pan and sputtered and hissed, dense unctuous fumes would billow out of the kitchen, attracting fat flies.

It was awful. But we could well understand ever since the day we couldn't take it anymore. On Monday our father had eaten sprats, and on Tuesday the house reeked of fatty tripe, and we thought this was too much of a good thing.

My brothers and I sat down at the table, pinching our noses shut, and tried to hold our breath as we chewed. We fanned fresh air at one another, but this air was also tainted. Then we told our father, "This is too disgusting for words."

It wasn't, though.

Our father had plenty of words. He raised his voice. He said that his father and mother hadn't had much during the war and had looked particularly at the outside of the cow out in the field because not too many cutlets and tender liver could be had from it.

"If we did get some meat on our plates," said our father, "it was the meat of a lesser cow, or a piece with a lot of fat on it. There wasn't an ounce too much on our bodies, so that fat was a good thing. Meat was meat, and we kept it in our mouths for a long time because who knew how long it would be, maybe weeks, before we'd chew on meat again. During the war, sprats were the codfish of the poor and fatty tripe was the steak. Sprats and tripe saved my life because once when my mother and father and I didn't think we'd make it to the end of the week without dying of hunger, we got a packet of fish from a fisherman and a butcher gave us a packet of tripe. That was lucky for us and just in time, too. And now I don't want to hear another word about it!"

We understood.

We looked at our plates where all kinds of things had gotten cold and heard our hearts beating.

"So, if I understand it right," said my one brother softly, "we wouldn't be around if the sprats and the tripe hadn't been around."

"Uh ... right," said our father.

"Uh ... right," we said, and from then on we thought my father should eat whatever he wanted. Brains, too, or udder.

BACK TO NORMAL

They were meeting above me. It was a Meeting of the Black Trousers. You could tell from the silence how important this meeting was. My brothers were silent and my father whispered. The chairs were neatly lined up around the table, and the room couldn't tolerate a lot of light. The door to the kitchen was closed. On the table, a stubby candle flickered, the first of the four flames on the wreath. Today Advent had begun.

"No turkey," said our father.

No turkey, I thought. I lay down on my back and spread out my arms and legs. I looked at the underside of the tabletop and turned my head sideways so the symbols that the carpenter had written on the plywood with a thick black marker ran straight. Sometimes the O was a zero and the v just a smudge. Sometimes I saw the sun with a bird beside it. Today they were letters. An O and a v. I pronounced them soundlessly, the one large, the other small, and touched my lips to feel which letter I liked more. Both, because I liked many things when I lay under the table and heard the buzzing over my head.

"No pie," said our father.

No pie, I thought. I could tell from our father's legs that he was presenting new subject matter. He placed his feet under his chair. As if this were a sign, my brothers' and our mother's feet also started moving. A lot of brothers were sitting on one foot, so it seemed as if they had only one leg. Our mother stuck her feet out, almost put them on my hand. Only Memée's feet stayed where they had been the whole time—beside each other on the floor, two blue slippers with clumps of ostrich feathers on them.

Under the table, the life of our mother and Memée, of our father and my brothers, was different from the way it was above the table. When my plate was empty and there was only going to be talk about things that had four syllables, I would often carefully slide off my chair and disappear below the edge of the tablecloth. Sometimes I was a fish. Sometimes I stayed myself. I played which legs belonged to which voice. Or I didn't play, and then I'd hum along with the drone of the voices a little bit. Sometimes I found that lying down was enough.

Today I looked the trousers down. Right above my head lay the Black Trousers, spread out as always, because that's the way it should be at a Meeting of the Black Trousers. I thought the table away, I thought the table away very hard, so that the trousers fell on top of me, and the candle and the papers on which our father and my brothers noted down important decisions did too.

"No tree," said our father.

No tree, I thought. I turned my head to the left and to the right, because all around me the chairs were being pushed back and my brothers and our mother and father got up and walked to the other room. Only Memée's slippers remained.

"Don't worry," she said to me through the tabletop. "They're going to see where the Christmas tree is going to be put this year, if there's going to be a tree."

"It's going to be a branch with oranges on it," I said. "We're going to do it differently from last year."

I heard Memée sigh. One slipper went up a little bit.

She meant that nothing was going to change. Every year we had to say that we were going to do it differently from last year. No turkey. No pie for dessert. No tree in which the baubles that had been dulled by time had to hang out of sight. But at the end of every Meeting of the Black Trousers, my brothers and our mother and father changed their minds like leaves on a tree. Always. Everything might as well be the way it had been, they'd say.

"Are you cold?" asked Memée.

"No," I said, and I listened to the voices in the other room. I rolled on my side and gave my bare legs a quick rub.

"It won't be long now," said Memée. "They'll be done with their meeting and you'll have your trousers back. Then everything will be back to normal."

LOSING

We were playing who could hold his breath the longest. My one brother won. That he was the oldest, had the biggest lungs and the biggest mouth, nobody said anything about that. My brother was celebrated.

At breakfast he was allowed to choose what game we'd play at the table. He picked something he thought up on the spur of the moment and explained very unclearly, and that's why he won another time. After that he thought of a game that he called hailstone sprinkles, but that wasn't a real game to me, although it did produce a nice effect on the tablecloth.

Then it was time to go to school.

In the hallway, there was a lot of traffic for a couple of minutes. Our mother and Memée had eyes in the backs of their heads and not enough hands. They saw anything that wasn't on straight or still hadn't been buttoned. They arranged things with their mouths, stroked and wiped, and herded my brothers in the direction of the door. My brothers had to cross the threshold, still had to give kisses, and then had to spend ten minutes on their bikes. It was none too soon. The school bell was just about to ring.

"Careful," said Memée as she clutched at her chest.

My brothers didn't do careful. Entire races had been lost because of it.

Our mother and Memée held me close a last time. I only had to go a few steps and then cross a little bridge and I'd be there. The nun was never upset if I came late. Welcome, welcome, she always said from behind the puppet stage or from above the banjo, and she'd nod at our mother that she understood.

I gave Memée a kiss. I heard her moan because she had to bend down, or maybe it was because she felt ashamed about so much shouting in the distance. She saw my brothers just like I did, the six of them racing down the street. Their bikes tilted from side to side the way cyclists' did in the final sprint. The finish line probably wasn't far away. Probably my one brother or my other brother would win, somewhere past the bend, and whoever was first would be allowed to choose where the next race began and how long it would be.

"Those boys," said Memée.

I looked at my brothers, the way they disappeared from view. Their fun made my thoughts dark and of the complaining kind. I never won anything, I was never once the first one—that kind of thought.

My mother had an eye for what you couldn't see.

She ran her hand over my head and said, "Shall we play who's the first to the nun's?" She was already off and running, but she wasn't doing too well because she still had her house slippers on and was laughing too hard to have any breath left over for speed.

I beat her. Child's play.

"Hooray!" cried the nun.

"Bravo!" shouted our mother.

"Sure," was all I said, because my thoughts remained dark. I took my seat in the classroom and looked at the banjo until the nun made sound come out of it and the door closed behind my mother.

After the lunch bell, it was noticeable that most of the mothers and fathers were having races, to tease me. They lifted their child in the air the highest or thought of something else in which you had to be the best or first.

I tried not to see it. In my mind, I was practicing how I would come home. I'd slam the door. I'd complain. I wouldn't give anybody a kiss. Each kind word I'd swat away from my ear. I'd sit at the table and stare at my plate until my brothers got home from school, until everybody was sitting at the table, until dinner was served, and I'd let everything that ended up on my plate get cold, even if I heard that my brothers were having a race, who'd be the first to clean his plate.

When I really did get home and slammed the door, nobody was impressed. To my surprise, the neighbor lady came out of the kitchen. She reached out her hands toward me, clutched me close, went and sat down in Memée's empty recliner, holding me in her arms. She said, "Now, listen. Calm down. Stop pushing. Sweetheart, something's happened. Nobody knows yet. I have to tell you."

She told me.

She said, "Terrible, isn't it?"

I said, "Yes. Terrible."

But I had no need to cry. I heard my brothers riding up on their bikes and throwing them against the garage door, and I startled myself because I felt my face brighten. My brothers yelled that they were first, but I mumbled, "No, you're not. You're not the first."

I raced to the mudroom, threw open the door and my arms too. I yelled that something had happened and that I knew what it was, that I was the first to know, and I shouted what had happened and jumped up and down, cheering.

But I wasn't celebrated. Nobody said that I was allowed to choose what game we'd play next. Not that gray day and not the next gray day. Later, when the days cleared up again, nobody even remarked on it. My brother won at running up the stairs and my other brother at cracking nuts. That I had been the first to know that Memée had died, nobody said a word about that.

ONE BROTHER WITH A LONG NAME

Once a year our father would stand at the bottom of the stairs and call our names up the stairway in a single breath as if we were one brother with a long name. The name stung us like a hornet, all seven at once. We'd lurch up, jump out of bed, pull our pajama bottoms up to our armpits, and stumble downstairs like one brother with fourteen arms and legs.

In our father's study the miracle had happened. It was impossible for us to simply look at it; we had to behold the treasure house whose door we'd thrown open, that was the feeling we had. There was so much that clamored for our attention that we first had to get used to the whole of it before we could start in on the white and the yellow and the pink of the sweets or on all the things that sparkled. Some treasures we tried not to see right away—the gloves, the piggy banks, the storage boxes—but after a while, we would be panting over even the useful things because there was always some tasty chocolate inside or underneath.

We sighed as if through one mouth. The almond letter cookies lay scattered up to our feet, here and there the gold of chocolate coins gleamed, and inside and underneath the bookcase and on the recliner lay building blocks and roller skates and roofing tiles and walkie-talkies and little trees and cars in bubble plastic. The miracle was explained then and there by our mother.

"Saint Nicholas was here," she'd say.

"And his dappled horse," we'd say, pointing at the family pack of marzipan that was missing a large piece and bore the imprint of large teeth.

"That's ... ," our father said, but didn't finish his sentence.

"All very, very nice once again," said our mother.

"Yes, very, very nice," we said. "Thank you, Santa."

We tried to pay attention to our faces, to whether the expression on them was grateful enough. We made little fists of our hands and stuck them behind our backs so that Saint Nicholas, if he should see us from somewhere up there, wouldn't think that we lacked manners or were greedy. We wondered out loud if his helper, Pete, had emptied the glass of beer and if the horse had been able to finish off the turnip and the carrot after the marzipan.

We settled down near the toys that were intended for us. It was always exactly what we'd asked Santa for. I found the next-to-biggest box filled with building blocks, and a printing kit I wanted to print my own stationery with—I'd already decided that before, when I was hovering over the little photograph in the toy catalog with a magnifying glass.

We sighed with contentment and felt our own and one another's toys with our eyes. One brother was strapping on his roller skates, another was figuring out how the batteries had to go into the walkie-talkie, and yet another imitated the brakes of a truck that was veering around a pile of marshmallow Mother Mary treats. Now and then one brother softly asked another what Santa had brought him.

"A walkie-talkie."

"A walkie-talkie!"

"Two, actually."

And then the other brother would look worriedly at his feet and sigh with relief because he had gotten roller skates and luckily two of them as well.

"Just look," our mother would say. She would stand with her arms folded, leaning against our father. If you looked closely, you could tell that they were glad. This year Santa had divided everything well, they thought. This year Santa hadn't made any mistakes.

They would leave us in the treasure house and sit down to breakfast together. They talked in soft voices and made hardly any sound when they put their coffee cups down.

Outside it would grow light, and with the light the miracle seemed less. My brothers and I would regain our voices. We'd go to the table and lay our toys in our laps or beside our plates, where they were in the way. My one brother would have words about this with the brother who was sitting beside him. My other brother would start arguing with my one brother because he wasn't allowed to touch the red button of the first walkie-talkie or the second one would blow up.

"Will not."

"Will too."

My one brother would land a punch and receive the swat of a roller skate in return.

It wouldn't be long before our father stood up. He'd call out our names in a single breath, as if we were one brother with a long name. Santa should hear us now, he'd say, adding that we had already spoiled next year's miracle because of our bickering.

We would fall silent at once. We would do what we could to retain the name of the brother with the long name, but by lunchtime, over turnip and carrot stew, we would already be sitting at the table like seven separate brothers, with our own names and our own arms and legs.

If we didn't hurry up and make sure we had our coats and our scarves on, and if we didn't go outside on the double, our mother would sell us to the first passer-by, because she had had enough of us, more than enough, the way we were always looking for trouble indoors.

No sooner was one of our arms in a sleeve than the doorbell rang. My brothers and I stiffened. Our mouths went dry on the spot. We glanced sideways at our mother to see if she was expecting somebody, somebody with a truck who caught children.

Our mother said nothing. She only snorted a few times.

We slowly sank down wherever we were and made ourselves small—against the wall, behind the stair railing, on a chair. We felt at our hearts to see if we couldn't get them to quiet down.

When the door swung open, we breathed a sigh of relief because it turned out to be the farmer woman who came by every week. She held out this week's butter, gave it to our mother, and said "Hi, boys" to us. She asked if we already knew that the firemen were going to take to the ice today. She wasn't absolutely sure, but it was very likely. It had been freezing hard for seven days already, and it didn't look like we'd be burning any less firewood the coming week.

"They have to try out the ice," said the farmer woman. "Ice is slick, everybody knows that, but you can fall through a thin patch pretty quick. It wouldn't be the first time."

"That's true," said our mother, and she waited a moment because the farmer woman was storing up air behind her cheeks and it looked like another story was about to follow.

Nothing came out, though. Inside it was getting just as cold as out.

We looked from our mother to the farmer woman, who shifted from one foot to the other and half turned around by way of beginning her homeward journey. She still had to say "Good day!" as she always did before she went, after which she could go. She poked her elbow at the air.

"Until next week, then?" said our mother.

"Yes," said the farmer woman. "Yes." She felt with her glove whether her mouth was still open and in a single breath launched into the story she had been chewing on—did our mother actually know that the farmer woman had lost her favorite cat under the ice shortly before the drama about the women last year? And did we still remember—that after the thaw, they had found two women, an old woman and her retarded sister, did we remember that?

"They were found hand in hand, but with their arms crossed, as if they'd tried to keep skating underwater. Seems they still had their hats on."

"That's what they say," said our mother, and we heard

her voice change as if her throat had frozen. She placed a period after her sentence with her nose. "Let's think of nice things," she said.

"Yes," said the farmer woman. "Ice is fun, that's true. Winter's the last."

Our mother had no ears for what was last about winter.

"Thank you," she said, and with a sweep of her hand closed the door and stood there for a while as if she were looking at the farmer woman through the wood.

We heard her breathe slowly. Her breath quivered.

"That wasn't polite of me," our mother said to herself.

We weren't sure whether she still remembered that we were around. We thought about letting her know we were still there by coughing a discreet little cough, but we didn't arrange anything and all coughed at the same time.

She didn't move a muscle.

It was a while before she lifted her head and looked at us. She said once more that it had not been polite of her. But there was no way around it. The farmer woman had been saying for ten years that she had lost her favorite cat under the ice, and for ten years the women had gotten caught under the ice last year. Starting a few winters ago, more and more details that had become more and more ludicrous had been added.

"They still had their hats on. How on earth did she come up with that?"

"How on earth?" we said, and we looked at one another. We pulled ourselves to our feet by the banister, smoothed our coats, and put on our hats.

The swishing of the nylon seemed to awaken our mother from a dream. She blinked her eyes and stuck out her lower lip. "Where are you all going?" she asked.

"Outside," we said. "On the double."

"Is that so?" said our mother. "To the canal, I'll wager. If you don't hurry up and make sure you take off your coats and hang your scarves on the coat rack and if you're not sitting in the kitchen on the double, I'll roll you up in a carpet and hand you over to a truck driver," because it was terrible, after all, the way we were always looking for trouble outside.

We looked at her to see if she meant it.

"We weren't planning to go on the ice," we said.

"You got that right," said our mother. "Under it."

She pointed an insistent finger at the kitchen. "That way," she said, and she ordered us to sit on the floor and on the counter and on the cupboards and the one stool. We were to sit quietly. We were to quietly watch her make pancakes for us, and we were not to ask why she was doing that in the middle of the morning because there was no because.

I said I had seen fire falling from the roof of the hospital, and got an elbow in my face.

"Does it hurt?" my brother asked. "Does it hurt?"

"No," I said as I rubbed my nose. "No." And I said that he didn't have to ask twice, I'd heard him. And hitting me in the face like that? He certainly didn't need to try that again because I knew of people who had gone blind after getting an elbow between the eyes, and some had also been brain-damaged. "A short circuit," I said as I pointed from his arm to my forehead. "They suddenly forgot everything they knew and could only talk nonsense."

"Nonsense," said my brother. "A short circuit. Well, you don't have much to lose from a short circuit and you already talk nonsense without even trying." He turned his back to me, bent down to engage his bicycle light, and sighed, before cycling on.

I grabbed the hem of his jacket, placed my fists in his sides, and lurched back a little when we started off. I pressed my lips together, looked away from my brother, and thought about the fire I had seen falling from the roof of the hospital.

"Roll up your tongue before you say anything," my brother said over his shoulder. He entered a curve so that the hospital in the distance was no longer beside us but almost in front of us and not so far away anymore. "Think for a minute if what you're going to say makes any sense. You'll see; if you think before you say something, you'll hold your tongue without even trying."

I looked at the back of my brother's head. My brother had started off the day muttering and he wasn't planning to end it whistling. While making his sandwich and wet-mopping the kitchen, he had sighed, in the supermarket he had groaned, and while playing blackjack, which he always liked doing, he had rolled his eyes.

Two people playing blackjack is just about the same as playing Ping-Pong by yourself. But it wasn't my fault nobody else was around.

"It's not fair," I said to my brother's back. "I saw fire fall from the roof of the hospital, and I get an elbow in my face."

I should have rolled up my tongue, then and there, on the back of the bicycle. My brother had been yelling at everybody all day already, at me for thinking a jack was a king, at our father who had gone to work, at our mother who had been lying in the hospital for three days already, and at our brothers who, since yesterday, had the same thing our mother did, although the doctors still weren't sure about that.

He cursed. Without any warning, he clenched his handbrakes and came to a halt right in the middle of the bicycle path. I flew into his back.

"Stop it," he said. "Stop it!" He looked around at me and with one hand pointed at the hospital in the evening sunlight. "So, where's the fire? I don't see anything burning. The roof's still in one piece. The windows are still in place. I don't hear any fire sirens anywhere. So, where's the fire?" He shook his head and moved his hand back and forth beside his ear. "Maybe I should hold my tongue," he said. "But I'm going to say it anyway. You get jaundice from being tired. And I'm tired. You should know that. Any day now I'll have jaundice, too, and you'll be the only one who doesn't."

"Oh," was all I could manage, but further reflection on what he meant was not possible. We had to look up, at our names being called.

Standing in front of a window on the seventh floor was our mother. It looked like she had less jaundice than yesterday—she was waving both hands at the same time.

My brother and I waved back. Our hands stopped in midair.

Above her head, two floors higher up, were our brothers. You could tell that it still wasn't certain if they had jaundice or not. But then, they weren't worried about it either. They waved at us, they waved rolls of toilet paper and showed us the matches they had found.

I rolled up my tongue. Rolled it up again. And then I said only what was strictly necessary. I said that I was going to walk the last stretch. That way my brother wouldn't get so tired.

QUIET

She drove a tiny van that was her size. Beside her there was room for her husband—at least if the husband wasn't too big. She couldn't fit any children; her bag was in the back.

Before seven in the morning she would arrive, and as soon as she had hung up her coat, she would start on the everyday sounds as if she were going down a list. The coffee grinder, the little gas water heater and the tap, the kettle on the flame, the bucket out of the closet. Nothing happened out of turn.

She never said a thing. It wasn't necessary, though, because everything spoke for itself. When we came downstairs, the table would be neatly set with exactly the right plates and the heavy spoon our father preferred to all the others, and the mug with the bear on it for my one brother because he had won that mug and nobody else was allowed to drink from it.

We ate in silence; this happened without even trying. The help didn't say much, but her body was not to be misunderstood. Even my brothers, who sometimes had big mouths, sealed their lips whenever she looked at them. She would lower the sock she was darning to her lap, raise her eyebrows, and wait. If she crossed her arms as well, she was punctuating what her body was saying.

Only when our father came out of the bathroom and, freshly shaven, took a seat at the table did we dare say anything. Never very much, and certainly not something with an opinion in it, because there had been a few times already when the help had said with her body that it was better if we kept our comments to ourselves. The time, for instance, when my one brother had said to my other brother that our mother's color would fade only if she lay flat on her back long enough. And that she would come home when all the yellow had left her face.

"Another week or so," my one brother had said.

The help had thought that was quite enough. She had lowered her sewing and made an exclamation point of her sigh so that my brother had looked at her slightly startled, forgetting what he wanted to say.

We didn't think the help kept quiet for nothing. She kept quiet because she was afraid of what might escape her, afraid that she might say something she didn't want to say. We thought she was jealous. She couldn't stand our talking with such caring about our mother because she wasn't a mother herself. She had no children to make breakfast for or to darn socks for. She had no boys who thought a week was a long time, because two weeks without our mother had already gone by and the time had dragged on as if we'd had to get through those days in oversized hiking boots. She kept quiet to be safe; that way she couldn't say anything wrong.

We didn't get a chance to play cops and robbers somewhere after dinner. No sooner had the table been cleared than out came the bag and the box. Snip, snip, the help's fingers called, and shame on us if we dared make motions different from hers. Out of the bag she poured seven children's scissors, and out of the box came pieces of curtain and worn-out blouses, pants, and pillowcases and a summer sweater and also a piece of corset without stays. Snip, snip, her fingers called again, and she fluttered around with pieces of cardboard we had to use as shapes.

The brothers who sometimes had big mouths didn't protest. If, late at night, we asked them why not, they said they kept quiet the way the help kept quiet. They kept quiet to be safe; that way they couldn't say anything wrong.

After a while, nobody opened their mouths at all anymore. We counted the days. We glowered at the help from under our eyebrows and made it clear with our bodies what we thought of her. We let the corners of our mouths droop, we hunched our backs, we pulled in our stomachs—that was what we thought of her.

It was a good thing that we mostly kept our mouths shut, for when the help left and didn't have to come back, she walked over to her little van and pulled out a big package. She tore the paper off and showed us a patchwork quilt. She said something in words. She said that we had made the quilt ourselves. It was a little present for our mother, who was better again. She pointed at us and at the scraps of curtains, blouses, pants, pillowcases, and a summer sweater, and also a piece of corset without stays.

LOOSE CHANGE

During the night from Sunday to Monday, our house was demolished. No crane was needed for this. Three men went up to the attic with their sledgehammers and started their work there. They knocked the tiles off the roof, hammered the walls to the floor, smashed the doors to smithereens. Nothing remained whole.

I stayed by the closet to see how they started on the first floor, making a hole in the floor through which they dumped the debris. By the time they had to start on our living room, the sky above us was blue and there was no living room anymore, because in the place where we had always sat around the fireplace now lay beams and bricks with the wallpaper from all the rooms on them.

I stood on top of the debris and asked the three men if they liked doing this. They said, "No, no. We think it's awful. Nobody likes to tear down a house. Treasure is what keeps us going. Gold in the gutter. A chest in a chimney. A box in a nook. And aside from that, there's always lots of loose change."

"Loose change?" I asked.

"Money that's fallen out of pockets over the years, was never picked up, and accidentally got swept under the base-

153

boards or into a crack between the floorboards. Any idea what all of that eventually amounts to?"

"No," I said, and I tried to imagine it.

I saw our mother with her broom, I saw our father with his wiping feet, and I kept hearing more and more money disappear under the baseboards, until it turned into a lot of money, not to say a heap. I wasn't able to breathe for a few seconds from the thought alone. I almost couldn't find the switch to the nightlight.

My brothers woke up grumbling, grunted like pigs, and rubbed their faces in their pillow as if it were a warm breast. They didn't want to know what was wrong. They didn't wonder why I was looking for my slippers in the middle of the night. We all left our beds sometimes, to pee or to get a glass of water.

I got down on my hands and knees and pushed my cheek against the floor. Looking under the baseboard didn't work very well. My eyes were too high up, even when I lay flat on my stomach. I rubbed my body against the linoleum, wishing the floor would turn into sand so I could dig a hole in it.

My one brother came and hung his head down, his face above my ear.

"Lost your marbles?" he said from my bed.

From the corner of my eye I saw the faces of my other brothers appear. They looked down at me and shook their heads.

"Did he have any, then?" they said to my one brother.

I turned over on my back and looked up, but past their ears. I said that they probably wouldn't find it interesting. No, of course they wouldn't find it interesting. By chance I had had a vision of loose change, but, oh well, what did a whole lot of money mean to them.

"Not a thing, right?" I said, and I shrugged my shoulders and turned my back on my brothers in the same motion, after which I counted to three.

At two, the first brothers fell like sandbags from the sky. Their breath came out of their lungs all at once so they had to nudge me to ask for more of an explanation, because they were too excited to get any words out.

"What did you say just now, what did you say?"

I said nothing. I smiled at my brothers, raised my index finger, and pointed at the baseboards. There, right in front of my nose, was a coin for the picking. I'd discovered it not a second ago. It was copper. It wasn't much, but it proved that I still had my marbles. I inched my finger in the direction of the money and poked it out with my longest fingernail. I held it up between thumb and forefinger, along with some dust and a bit of black goop.

"Wow," said my brothers in unison.

"Yes," I said, glad they understood me.

But my brothers didn't understand me. They lay there shaking their heads, avoided my eyes, and went back to bed. They laughed at me and said foreign words to one another so I didn't belong.

There was no need for me to belong. I stayed on my back

until my brothers had been asleep for a long time. The next day I found a couple of coins that were the beginning of a million. I twisted the money into a piece of paper and I let it slip down behind a baseboard. Now nobody could reach it anymore. In the note, I kindly greeted the men who would one day tear down our house. I wrote that I hoped that they were happy with their find. After that, I started on my own fortune, looking in the other rooms: half a stamp, one of our mother's bobby pins, a thumbtack, part of a newspaper headline that read *Untouchable!*, a piece of chewing gum that had lost its flavor, and now and then a few copper coins.

THE CREATURE

Just before seven, even before the alarm in our father and mother's room went off, we got up and sneaked down the stairs behind one another. We dreamed together in the lost hallway, a little room three feet square that had no purpose, with the kitchen door on one side and the basement door on the other.

My one brother said we had to be quiet.

"Don't wake him up," he whispered, and by that he didn't mean our father.

We fell silent at once. We pressed our lips together and could already smell a little of our cold sweat.

Carefully my one brother opened the basement door. He first wanted to make sure that nobody was standing behind the door. Only then did he look over his shoulder and give us a serious nod. Did we smell the breath of the creature already, he asked, and did we feel its coldness?

"Yes," we said, because of course we felt that blanket of coldness fall over us. A hint of smoke or gas penetrated our noses. The smell made our thoughts gray as if our brains were dying off.

"Careful on the stairs," said my brother. He was the first

to disappear into the gaping dark of the basement, and we followed on his heels, although we shuffled. We held on to one another's pajama tops and bottoms. The wall was cold, and on the other side there was a lot of emptiness but no railing.

Our eyes needed some time to get accustomed to the dark. When they were used to it, we still didn't see much. Instead we looked with our noses. We smelled the closet with the homemade jam and canned pears. We smelled the rack holding our father's old papers. We smelled the farthest corner where the heavy table with the plastic tablecloth on it stood. In that corner, dust made it tickle way up in our noses and it stank the most of sweet and sour. Under the table was where we had to be. There was no safer place.

"Now cut it out," said my one brother when we were all sitting down. We didn't know what he was talking about, so we stopped what we were doing. We stopped scratching, we stopped shivering, breathing, being scared.

My brother said that we were strong together, which was nice to hear. Nobody felt like a hero all by himself. Our flesh grew together on the spot so that after a while we sat under the table like one brother, peering into the dark with bated breath.

Above our heads we heard the shrill of the alarm clock and our father stumbling around. We knew that the danger had woken up with the alarm. It heard just like we did the way our father walked around the bed and pulled up the window blinds. In another second or two, we knew, he would put on his slippers. Now the pit-pat of Father's feet on the linoleum changed into soft droning thuds that might have made the steps of the stairs creak but otherwise remained almost inaudible if you listened carelessly.

We cringed and didn't dare breathe.

"Pay attention, now," my brother whispered.

We nodded carefully. We looked at our own eyebrows. Right above our heads we heard our father at the top of the stairs. He took the first five steps down, turned the corner, and started down the long stairs.

"Don't be scared," my brother whispered.

We shook our heads and tried to count our father's steps, how many he needed to reach the door to the living room. We waited with racing hearts for a squeaking hinge, for the clink of a latch, for the one click we heard every cold morning when our father turned the thermostat to seventy.

"Now!" said my brother.

Every muscle in our bodies tensed. In the dark of the basement, the creature leapt up with a barking sound as if a powder keg had blown open. Its one square eye flared up orange and bellowing, and the entire basement trembled and shook. We thought that the world was coming to an end. We opened our eyes wide; for long seconds we were scared to death that the creature would head our way, but it stayed where it was and warmed the whole house.

We smiled at one another with satisfaction, my brothers and I. Our faces glowed from the fire in the boiler. We could tell by looking at each other that we had been scared and had enjoyed it, and were now ready for a hearty breakfast.

THE WARM GIRL

One day a girl came to live with us. Our father said her name was Françoise. At first we didn't believe this was her real name. My one brother thought Father had called her that to be clear, because she spoke French. My other brother said it was a remedy for homesickness, because she'd have to speak our language for two weeks, and if she longed for her French home, she would still be able to comfort herself with a French name.

She looked a little bewildered when our mother and father and my brothers and I opened the door. She stood on the front steps as if she'd been put there by somebody who had quickly run away, and softly she said who she was.

"Françoise."

There you are, we thought. And as our father had requested, we all said, "Welcome, Françoise."

It sounded as if we were immediately giving lessons in our language because we also tried to act out what being welcome is. My one brother held his head to the side and smiled, my other brother clapped his hands, but most of my brothers pointed with outstretched arms in the direction of the living room, into which at that moment the cold wind was blowing.

Our mother was the most hospitable of all. She pulled Françoise into the hallway and started unwrapping her as if we had received her as a gift. Her hat came off, her scarf came off; her mittens and her coat she took off herself. Meanwhile, Mother made sure that Françoise learned all our names at the same time, so she forgot them all at the same time.

When she was standing there unwrapped and glowing in the living room, everybody was quiet for a few seconds. We thought at first glance that Françoise was something that fit with our heater. She had navy blue knit legs, and her dress was of thick red wool, and she had a ribbon in her hair that to us also seemed made of wool, but crocheted, with wooden beads in it. She was the warmest girl we had ever had over to the house.

"Françoise," said our father, pulling at his lower eyelid with his forefinger. He walked over to our mother and put his arm around her shoulders as he said her name. After that he pulled at his eyelid again and grabbed hold of my oldest brother. Françoise nodded when she heard his name, but I could tell she had forgotten it at the same time. My brothers didn't see. They were too busy standing most advantageously and winking. When they heard their names, they pushed their chests out, and if they had been able, they would have radiated light.

Françoise looked from one to the next and then looked around. I figured out right away that she was looking for a word. When she found it, she pointed at it.

"Tree!" she said, but she might as well have said *dream* or *three*, because that's how it came out of her mouth.

My brothers got very excited. They went over to our Christmas tree, nodding, and pointed at the baubles and tinsel and the spike on top, and they said all the words that occurred to them because they wanted to teach Françoise our language. *High* and *clock* and *star* and *holiday* they suddenly felt were important words.

Françoise became a little disheartened, and that's why I shrugged my shoulders and wiped the air with my hands. I drew a bag in the air into which I swept my brothers' words, and I simply exclaimed, "Hooray, the Christmas tree!" I had also shouted this the week before, when the tree had been put up, and everybody had fallen silent. This time, too.

Our father and mother and my brothers and I, we all looked at Françoise, who just looked at me and winked at me and smiled a huge smile.

"Hooray, the Christmas tree!" she said, and to my surprise, our father and mother started clapping. My brothers didn't clap. They growled, but I couldn't understand why.

Three days later I still didn't understand. My brothers had gone out of their way to teach Françoise our language. My one brother had made a drawing of a skate for her, with arrows and words, but the word for laces, for instance, she didn't remember. Another brother had ducked into the kitchen one afternoon to bake Françoise a cake, but she didn't acquire the words *egg* and *milk* and *sugar* from this. The harder my brothers tried, the fewer words she remembered.

After the turkey we had for Christmas dinner, which had progressed with many silences, I knew for sure. You had to keep things simple with Françoise and be clear. I crawled close to her on the sofa, put her heater arms around me, and said clearly, "Hooray, warm!"

Things like that she understood.

"Hooray, warm," she repeated.

I nodded and lay there while my brothers looked at me disapprovingly because they weren't very good at giving lessons.

"Hooray, Noël," Françoise said suddenly.

I nodded, even though I felt like saying that my name was different. But if you're lying there all warm, it's sometimes better to let a mistake be a mistake.

DISCARD

DATE DUE

FIC
MOE